BASIC GUITAR

edited by **JON SIEVERT**

The Guitar Player Basic Library
By the editors of Guitar Player Magazine

GPI Publications
Cupertino, California

HAL LEONARD PUBLISHING CORPORATION
8112 West Bluemound Road, Milwaukee, WI 53213

GPI BOOKS

Art Director
Dominic Milano

Production Manager
Judie Eremo

Designer
Christina Holt

Darkroom
Cheryl Matthews, *Director*
  Mark Medalie, Paul Haggard

Typesetting
Leslie Bartz, *Director*
  Birgit Byrd

Proofreader
Jerry Martin

Music Editor
Tom Darter

Editor: Guitar Player Magazine
Tom Wheeler

President/Publisher: GPI Publications
Jim Crockett

Associate Publisher: GPI Publications
Don Menn

Director: GPI Books
Alan Rinzler

PHOTO CREDITS

Cover: Design by Dominic Milano; photo
left: Jon Sievert; lower right: Keith
Richards by Neil Zlozower.

Page viii: George Grippon; 9: Christopher Parkening
by Gary Bakken; 10: Neil Zlozower; 33: Jon Sievert;
38: Peter Townshend by Neil Zlozower; 53: Jon
Sievert; 62, 63, 64: Jon Sievert; 78: John McLaughlin
by Wendi E. Lombardi; 81: B.B. King by Jon Sievert.

Library of Congress Catalog Card Number:
84 - 81995

ISBN: 0-88188-293-3

Printed in the United States of America

INTRODUCTION

Since our first issue back in 1967, *Guitar Player Magazine* has made it a policy to publish columns of information, inspiration and advice written by working professional musicians. Consequently some of the world's finest guitar players and teachers have written for *Guitar Player* over the years, contributing articles, columns and musical examples. This legacy has grown to be a tremendous library, a basic curriculum of educational material for the amateur or professional player.

Unfortunately most of the original issues which published this material have become out-of-print and unavailable for quite some time now. To preserve this original material, we have therefore launched The Guitar Player Basic Library: a series of definitive, fundamental volumes collected, edited, redesigned and reprinted, from the pages of *Guitar Player Magazine*.

Basic Guitar, a volume in this Guitar Player Basic Library, has a Foreword by Les Paul, with contributions from stellar performers Rik Emmett and Barney Kessel, teachers Jerry Silverman and Happy Traum, and many others. *Basic Guitar* has been designed to be a comprehensive, practical introduction to the technique and art of playing guitar—for those who are picking up the guitar for the first time, as well as for those who've already been playing a few years.

Each column in this book is an individual lesson offering many hours of work. Many columns also point the way toward exploring further in specific areas. Read. Study carefully and slowly over time. Practice, enjoy your explorations in the wide world of guitar.

Jon Sievert

Note: *You will see that the style of music notation changes occasionally from column to column. Since these articles are drawn from more than 10 years of* Guitar Player, *the production of the examples reflects the changing style of the magazine's music production department. In addition, the chord symbols used for specific chords change from article to article, reflecting the different usages of the author/artists. In all other respects, the differences between the examples are only cosmetic.*

FOREWORD

STARTING OUT THE RIGHT WAY

One way of learning to play music is for your parents to buy you an instrument, find you a teacher, and tell you, "Learn." You go take a lesson, the teacher assigns homework, mom or dad sees to it that you put your hour in every day, without paying any particular attention to what you're practicing. If you're not really interested in the instrument you put in your time, go back to the teacher unprepared, the teacher tells you to practice your lesson for another week, takes the money, and figures "What the hell!" I'm not putting all teachers into this category—there are many competent people who are teaching for reasons other than making a fast buck.

But another way of learning to play is to *want* to. Find a good teacher, and, as a starter, here are a few things to remember:

To *try* is very important.

Listen to your teacher; respect him or her along with the super-players—the pro's—they became super-players only after many years of hard work.

Be patient, and learn one thing at a time.

Don't worry about playing fast—this comes with practice. Start very slow, and gradually increase the tempo to as fast as you can play, remembering to keep everything clean and even. I repeat—*clean* and *even*. There are many ways of fingering and picking—this is where a teacher who is experienced can lead the student down the correct road. The way you practice your fingering and picking is crucial at the beginning—so many players find themselves trapped at a dead-end later on because of the way they practiced in the initial stages of learning.

What I do is hand the student a guitar—in tune—and let him familiarize himself with the sound. Then I lower a string several tones and ask him to tune it as he originally heard it. It's important for a teacher to know how good an ear the student has been blessed with, and to notice his sense of rhythm, reflexes and coordination, and his attitude. Just to *want* to play is not enough—a serious student must also have all the things just mentioned. The teacher must remember that the student is new to the game; we old-timers have been around for a long spell and have not only watched and studied with others, but have discovered the pitfalls involved and know what lies ahead.

At the beginning, I prefer an acoustic box with a decent, playable action and a medium pick; I start the student with all down-strokes until he gets the basics. I point out the do's and don'ts gradually. Don't move too fast. I like to mention to the student that he can't write a letter until he learns the ABC's.

After advancing to the electric guitar, play with the amplifier facing you—you can really fool yourself into thinking you're playing clean when you're not listening to a speaker pointed directly at you. You should hear yourself as an audience will hear you, and believe me, clean playing counts. Long, fast runs aren't going to impress anyone if the only reason you're playing them is to play a long, fast run. Make every note count—say something.

I've taught quite a few people in my lifetime, and I sure learned to teach the player what *not* to do. I really hand-tailored them, realizing that each student is different. It's very difficult, but the teacher must adjust to each student. If student and teacher click, this means the teacher really knows where it's at: Teaching the basic rudiments, slow and clean, keeping the student's hopes high; and exposing him to the best musicians. If possible, I take the student to watch the very best, in person, and also get tapes or records of these people. And you can bet that these players we go to see did the same thing—listened to those they admired, and learned something from everyone.

Sometimes a student will say he would like to play like "so-and-so," who may not be the best musician in the band, but the student unconsciously chooses him because he seems within the student's reach as a goal. Also, once in a while a student figures he's got it all after only a half-dozen lessons.

Another serious problem is when the teacher assigns a certain piece of music with proper fingering and picking, and the student practices incorrectly for a week, in spite of a God-given rhythm and a good ear. This is where patience on the teacher's part is important—he must realize that it takes many hours of practice to play well, and he must also make certain that he gets the message across to the student. A student and I were listening to a fine musician and the student said, "Let's go. I can't learn anything from him." Maybe *he* couldn't, but I did. I learned a mess of things—some what to do and some *not* what to do. The student's antenna must be kept raised—what good is a receiver without an antenna?

I was very fortunate to teach students who all had excellent ears, a good sense of rhythm, and the desire and will to learn the methods I suggested. I also got great satisfaction from teaching my sons to play. I'm proud to say that they're not only good musicians, but also excellent audio engineers, and they are winning awards for the sound they are achieving on phonograph records.

To sum it up, I again stress *clean* playing and *patience*. Some people learn faster than others, so don't try to exceed your capabilities. Play what you can play easily, and the speed and technique will come by itself. A really serious player won't have to be told to practice. He's got to realize that it's the only road toward perfection; and don't strive for absolute perfection—it's not to be had.

You will find that the more deeply involved you get with the instrument, the more things you will find that you want to learn—I don't think you can ever stop learning. Don't stay on one road—there are many exciting things happening in other branches of music than the particular type you may want to start with. Reading is very important if you want to become a versatile player, and it will open many new roads to you. Also, the more successful you become, the less time you will have for practicing, but you can learn from what's going on around you.

Never stop listening to other players, and if, at the beginning, you base your playing on someone else's style, there's nothing wrong with that; but don't stay there. Don't be a carbon copy. Try to extract the better things and incorporate them into your own style, always learning, always adding to your versatility.

In closing, I raise my beer in a toast: "Good luck, and many happy years of playing."

Les Paul

CONTENTS

1. BUYING AN INSTRUMENT

BUYING THE RIGHT GUITAR

Choosing a guitar is highly subjective. For instance, an instrument that sounds good to you might not sound good to your friend—and vice versa. One person may prefer a higher string action, a different color of wood, or a larger guitar. So who's right?

As you might have guessed already, the answer is no one, and everyone. But there are a few things *anyone* thinking about purchasing a guitar should do. First, take a friend along who knows about the instrument. (Many people probably have already told you this—*GP* certainly has many times—but it bears repeating.) Second, take plenty of time and try out a large selection of types and styles. Third, even after you have settled on a specific model, compare different guitars of that same model—two instruments can be made by the same manufacturer, with identical features and specifications, and *still* look, sound, and feel different.

Another important point to consider is what style of playing you want to learn. A guitar well-suited to fingerpicking may not necessarily be the best choice for, say, flatpicking.

When you have finally settled on *the* guitar (hopefully the dealer will be one of the many who know the instrument and want to help you make the best decision possible), look for a quiet place and play.

It's very difficult for anyone to hear what they sound like when someone across the showroom is testing out a trap set, and the person next to them is jamming on a banjo with a keyboardist who likes to turn up the organ's volume—all the while the phone is ringing off the hook. And, besides testing the guitar yourself, ask your friend to play it so you can hear how it projects—how it sounds to your listeners. Play it lightly and vigorously. Fingerpick it, flatpick it, and strum it. Test the sound all over the fingerboard. Take your time, and explore the instrument.

So now you have some idea of just how confusing buying a guitar can be if you are not prepared. Knowing what you're doing isn't difficult; it just calls for some attentiveness and expert advice. Speaking of which, our Advisory Board members who have commented in the pages that follow have given both subjective and objective opinions, and they have attempted to make clear which tips are personal preferences and which are more widely accepted. Also, there are many good suggestions about what to look for when buying *any* guitar in each section, so you should give every section a read—whether or not you are interested in purchasing that type of instrument.

With those thoughts in mind, the following article should enlighten those people new to the guitar as well as heighten the knowledge of more experienced players.

STEEL-STRING   DOC WATSON

Regardless if the guitar is "dolled up" or not, you should buy one that has a good tone and good action (that is, it should fret easily), and one that frets true. If the instrument is perfectly in tune but sounds discordant in certain positions when you play it, that means the intonation isn't right. But intonation is kind of hard to judge unless you know something about the guitar, so I suggest you bring someone with you who knows a *lot* about it.

You don't have to pay an arm and a leg for a decent instrument. A fine steel-string can run anywhere from $350 to $700. It won't have much trim on it, but it may well sound very nice.

One thing you'll want to consider before buying a guitar is the instrument's size. It should fit you. For instance, if you have small hands, you'll want one with a moderate size neck. As far as the body size goes, if you don't like or can't handle the big dreadnought, there is a concert model made by many companies that is a beautiful instrument for a young lady or fellow whose hands are small. But most people want the big guitar—one that has the real full sound. And you can't blame them—I wanted one when I first started playing. When I was 13 I had a Stella, and I yearned for a big old Martin. Finally, when I was about 17, I got out and picked a bunch in the street on Saturdays and saved up and bought me one.

New guitars aren't the only ones to buy. Remember, you can get a fine used instrument, but take someone with you who is experienced to look the guitar over. Usually, the used ones that are *really* good will have a price tag on them, however.

As far as the physical features on a guitar are concerned, I like steel-strings with adjustable necks or with truss rods in them to support the neck. Also, you should check all the seams where the binding goes on and see that it's put together well. Occasionally, they'll sneak something by you that will look good at first, but will come apart in a few days. To avoid this, look at all the joints on the guitar to see that the builder did a clean job with gluing. If it's sloppy, you better dodge it.

Because each guitar has its own sound characteristics, I don't really prefer one type of wood over another, with the exception of the top of the instrument: The vast majority of the good ones will have either a spruce or cedar top to sound right. As far as I'm concerned, I like both rosewood and mahogany, although maple is fine too. I play mahogany, but I have a good old Gallagher [J.W. Gallagher & Son, Wartrace, TN 37183] G-70 at home that's rosewood.

So to sum up, whether you buy a new or used, brand-name or obscure-name guitar, make sure that it sounds good and it's built well. Take along someone who knows about guitars when you first go to buy one—it could save you a big headache later. Always operate under the old caution thing: A guitar can look good and sound good, and then come apart in a few months. And above all, you people who are really into learning the guitar, you don't learn how to play it overnight. You have to practice like the devil. I didn't, and it took me a long time to ever get it to sound half like I wanted it to.

HOLLOWBODY ELECTRIC   CHET ATKINS

One of the most important things for a beginner to look for when choosing a guitar is the action, because when you first begin to play, your fingers tend to get sore if the strings are too high. What can result, I think, is that the person tends to get disgusted and maybe choose not to pursue practicing. Also, I think the best thing for someone who doesn't know much about the instrument is to take a good guitar player along when they go shopping. But even if you're an absolute beginner, *you* should make the aesthetic decisions: Choose an instrument that pleases you, one that looks good. The one great advantage I feel hollowbody guitars have is that they do have more "romance" than solid guitars; this may be a reason for the renaissance in their popularity.

I think a shopper should also run their hand up and down the neck to make sure that they don't get cut by a fret. If there are a lot of sharp frets, that usually means the wood has shrunk a lot, and the frets would need re-dressing. You can actually get hurt sometimes if the fret work is bad. To correct the problem, all you need is a flat file.

Always choose a guitar that is comfortable to play. Sit down and see if it "fits" you. A small person probably shouldn't go out and buy a Gibson Super 400 because they'll barely be able to reach around it. So if I had shorter arms, I think I'd get a smaller guitar. Scale is what matters anyway: For fingerpicking, I would prefer the 25½"scale, which is long, because I think it tends to stay more in tune when you're playing chords. When you push a string down to the fretboard, it alters the tuning slightly—and the shorter the neck, the greater the effect. So for fingerpicking and chord work, I prefer the long scale. People with short fingers, and beginners who usually play in the first position would probably prefer the shorter scale length.

If you're thinking about buying a used instrument, bring along a knowledgeable person. Some of the older instruments are very good, and you might be just as well off buying one of them. But sometimes they can have faults that only an experienced player or technician can see. Beware of warped necks, cracks, and necks pulled loose from the body. Sometimes, for instance, used instruments have been left in a car too long, and the glue melts and the neck pulls loose and it eventually glues itself back in a strange manner.

Concerning warranties, if a buyer finds two instruments that are apparently equal in quality, I feel that it would be to the buyer's advantage to buy the one with the longer warranty. But if it's just a guarantee on a very cheap guitar, then I feel you haven't gained anything by buying it.

I don't think there are all that many bad things that will go wrong with a guitar, if you take care of it properly. One of the greatest enemies of any wooden instrument is low humidity. For instance, when you get up north where it is very cold, the wood shrinks and splits. So in such climates it's always a good idea to humidify a guitar in some manner, such as sticking a wet sponge inside of, let's say, a 35mm film container with a few hole punched in it and putting it inside of a round-hole guitar. There are also these dampettes you can buy. I've also seen people cut apples and put them in their cases—I don't actually know how much good that does. Don't set your instrument close to radiators or leave them in cars. If it's very cold, it may crack the finish; if it's very hot, it may melt the glue. Also, keep people away from your instrument who don't know anything about it. These folks often will lean a guitar up against a wall—and they don't know how to do it right—and it may fall and possibly break the neck off. You should lean the guitar up against something down at the center of the neck, not up at the top.

While brand-name guitars are fine, I also think that some of the more obscure-name instruments are very good as well. The Japanese, for instance, can build a guitar—or just about anything—of whatever quality you want: bad, good, and in-between. Some of your best guitars, I think, are probably names that you don't hear much about because they are handmade or custom-made, but they are very expensive and not usually in a beginner's price range.

If you get a really *bad* guitar, like I first had (the neck was busted loose and the action was about 1/2" high, which is *real* high), you can still learn to play in spite of that. Also, I think that people should learn to play by ear first off, because that gets rid of most people with no talent. I'm kind of joking now, but there is some validity to my point. I certainly don't wish to downgrade the ability to read music—it's sure been a great help to me; it gave me so much more confidence when I was able to read—and I suggest that everyone eventually learn how to do it.

For all you guitarists, beginning, and advanced, remember that there are no short-cuts to learning how to play. It takes practice, practice, practice. You have to have a passion for the guitar, and that's something that either you have or you don't. I know I slept with my guitar, took it to school—just about everywhere. So you have to have that desire in you.

FLAMENCO   JUAN SERRANO

If the student is a beginner and doesn't know the difference between a very good flamenco guitar and an intermediate or cheap instrument, he or she should buy a guitar that is not very expensive. Some people may think it's a cheap move, but you should buy it anyway—you never know whether as a beginner you are going to continue being interested in playing. Sometimes after only a few weeks the student discovers how difficult it is and quits.

Over the past few years, the economics in this country and in Spain changed a lot. You would have to spend perhaps $100 and up for a beginner's guitar now, since you can't find one for $40 or $50 like you used to. When you decide that you need to buy a really good guitar, I always recommend that you buy the best, because you'll have it forever. You don't have to spend $400 or $500 for an intermediate guitar only to discover one or two years later that you need a better one—this is the way you start to spend money.

Normally, I recommend that the flamenco guitar be made of cyprus. It is a lighter color than the classical guitar—the classical is usually made of rosewood, dark wood, while cyprus is very light. Some of the guitars made in this country are light, but they're made of another kind of wood—not cyprus. And the string action has to be very close to the neck for flamenco, because this is necessary in executing the various techniques. Another difference between the flamenco and the classical guitar is the inclusion of a tap plate (golpeador) on the former. Also, I make sure that the guitar's tuning heads are thick wood, not machined metal. (The choice of wood over metal in this case is one of keeping with tradition instead of a matter of quality—there are several excellent machined metal tuners.)

If you want a handmade custom guitar, which I consider to be the best, you have to think in terms of spending between $1,200 and $1,500 minimum. I remember when one of my students went to Spain and came back and said, "I just bought a beautiful guitar for $500." I said, "From whom?" Then he tells me the name of the maker and I say, "But that is not custom-made, because such guitars are never already finished—you have to put in an order." There is a good guitar maker in Cordova, for example, who will make you a guitar, but you'll have to wait six or seven years to get it.

When I order my own guitars, I always tell the maker what kind of action I want, the type of wood to be used in the body, etc., because I know what to look for—I have been playing for years. So if a person is a beginner, he or she should seek the advice of a professional and ask that person or someone else who is knowledgeable about guitars to go along, because if you don't really know *anything*, the salespersons can say whatever they want and you won't know the difference. For instance, a salesperson might say that this guitar is better than that one because the first costs $50 more, and the student might think, "It must be better if it is more expensive"—but maybe it *isn't*. A person with knowledge about guitars will be able to tell if a particular instrument is good from the quality of the tone, the action, and other things.

Also, some students only look for the beautiful instrument, but that's merely cosmetics—one should not look solely at the beauty of the guitar. Instead, one should be more concerned with important things like the sound quality and action. (Keep in mind that action, which involves string height, can be adjusted.) And always remember, even if two guitars are made by the same person, using the same wood and everything, the instruments *will* be different. So for beginners I recommend that you, with the help of a professional or someone who knows about guitars, should try a variety of instruments which are inexpensively priced before buying.

SOLIDBODY ELECTRIC   JEFF BAXTER

Buying a guitar is like buying a car—everybody has different reasons for choosing one over another. Not everybody purchases a car solely for transportation, and so it is with an electric guitar; few people buy one only for its ability to function as an electric guitar. One thing to avoid, however, is just walking in the store and automatically paying list price for any guitar. To be sure, there is nothing wrong with buying a brand-name instrument, but I feel that when you see a $1,500 price on a guitar, and you're only making $150 a week in a shoe store, it seems that one would want to seriously consider the possibility of buying a lower-priced instrument, or seeking a discount on the expensive one.

Another important point to consider: *Why* do you want to buy a certain guitar? If you want to stand up in front of people so that they can see that you have a nice-looking instrument—if you believe that that will give you some sort of credibility—that's one thing. But you can save a lot of money and actually have some fun by going out and purchasing a guitar that *plays* right.

After shopping around for an instrument and deciding which is right for you, you should perform a few simple tests before making the purchase final. First, plug the guitar onto an amp and turn up the volume on both; then wiggle the guitar's output jack around and listen for any noise. In both cases, there should be silence (with the exception of the amp's hum). Also, turn the guitar's controls slowly listening again for noise; a crackling may mean that the controls are dirty, and while the problem is easily rectified, you still might be able to use it as a bargaining point.

Besides checking the electronics, you might want to be aware of the guitar's scaling length, or the length of the fingerboard. Some people prefer a short scale because they like to be able to bend the strings a little easier (the shorter the scale the less tension there is on the strings, all other things being equal.) However, a player who prefers single-string lines or fingerpicking may well appreciate a long scale more; not only does the guitar seem to spread the harmonics over the pickup a lot better, but it also offers a little more string tension.

Another important factor to consider when buying a guitar is its intonation, or how well it stays in tune when played in different chord positions up the fingerboard. But you should ask a fairly experienced player of repairperson to help you out on this one.

When I'm looking for a nice used guitar—and you shouldn't rule out buying one—I try to find one that has the most grooves in the neck, especially around the first four frets. Of course, many people prefer the shiny, spotless look, but to me, extensive wear indicates that the person who had it before was a real stompin' rhythm player, and the guitar has been *played*. I feel that the more a guitar is played, and the more the wood on the guitar (whether solid or hollowbody) is vibrated, the better the instrument is going to be.

So remember, the name on the guitar doesn't *necessarily* mean much: it's how you like it that's important. The guitar is not supposed to be a status symbol—it is the tool of your trade.

CLASSICAL   LAURINDO ALMEIDA

Because a beginner would likely not know what to look for when purchasing a classical guitar—types of wood, action, intonation—he or she should always bring a friend along who knows about guitars.

Many students don't have much money, so they can expect to pay from $150 to $300 just for a relatively inexpensive guitar. But if they can pay more, a buyer has quite a variety of instruments to choose from, since there are so many makers these days. Two very important things to consider, which actually are closely related, are the strings and the bracing in the instrument. There is a difference between the 1st, 2nd, and 3rd (treble) strings and the three bass strings in terms of volume and vibration (the bass strings being much louder), and a good guitar will have internal bracing that balances the bass and treble sounds. Braces are made heavy on one side (bass) and light on the other (treble) to break the vibration of the bass strings. If the bracing is good, then you won't have a booming bass overpowering the treble sound: The instrument will be balanced.

Another important thing to look for is that the top of the guitar, or the soundboard, should be made of soft, porous wood like spruce or pine, while the back and sides of the instrument should be made of a very hard, compact wood like Jarcaranda (from Brazil) or other types of rosewood. You want the sound to go through the guitar's top, not the sides or back. Also, look at the tuning keys to make sure that they are very tight, because loose keys can cause irritating vibration when you play.

There is a great deal of difference in string action between a classical guitar and, let's say, a steel-string acoustic. The action on a steel-string is much too high for classical playing—it could cut your fingers (which is one reason you don't use steel strings on a classical instrument). Also, the fingerboard is narrower on a steel-string than on a classical guitar. Personally, I prefer a fingerboard that is wider than a steel-string's but narrower than the kind found on a regular classic guitar. My hands are small, and I have some difficulty in playing, for instance, a full-sized Ramirez classical. So my fingerboard is shorter than usual from the 12th fret to the nut, and that makes it very comfortable for me to play. It may be a minor thing, but things like that can make all the difference in the world.

A friend of mine has made me a single-cutaway classical guitar that I like very much. Its fingerboard, rather than joining the body at the 12th fret, joins at the 16th (on the treble side), giving me more notes and added flexibility. But while you can't buy a mass-produced cutaway classical guitar in the U.S. yet, the idea is a good one that might catch on.

Remember one thing: Buy as much guitar as you can afford. [*Ed. Note: See Juan Serrano's contribution to this article for a different viewpoint.*] If you purchase a very cheap guitar to start with, it's easy to lose not only money but also interest in the instrument. A cheap guitar will have little or no resale value—what you spent you will probably never recover when you want to move up to a better model, and many times a student will buy a cheap instrument and get discouraged and give up because the guitar is too difficult to play or doesn't sound good. The problem may be because the guitar itself is of inferior quality, not because the student is unable to learn how to play correctly and beautifully.

One other point that many people forget about when buying an instrument: If you plan on doing any traveling with your guitar, buy a good case for it, You can spend a lot of money for an instrument and neglect to protect it with a sturdy case, and the result is usually a broken or damaged guitar. I have a case so strong you could do a flamenco dance on it and the guitar would not be damaged. It cost me more than a regular case, but to me it's worth every penny if it keeps my major investment safe and playable.

compiled by Jim Schwartz

ACCESSORIES AFTER THE FACT

So you finally bought your first guitar. It's a beauty, isn't it? All nice and bright and shiny! Now, what else do you need to get yourself all set for your first plunk? There are several things, and I hope to give you an idea of what you'll need, and *why*.

Case. The guitar is one of the few instruments that I know of that you can buy and carry out of the store in a paper bag. And, believe it or not, I've seen it happen. Personally, I don't recommend it. There are several types of guitar covers and cases that are available; some are better than others. In ascending order we have:

The canvas bag is a thin cover of canvas or vinyl that fits like a glove over the guitar. It offers a marvelous protection against dust if you remember to close its BVD-like snappers at the bottom end. Otherwise, though, it's not too effective against table corners, doorknobs, and other solid objects. It is not recommended to be used outdoors on rainy days, either.

The cardboard case: Manufacturers like to call this "chipboard." For a not-too-expensive instrument—especially if a child has to lug it around—this is the ideal case (usually costing less than $20). With any kind of hard use, it's luggage-type clips will eventually hold less and less effectively, so be careful about the guitar falling out. It does offer a fair amount of protection against *reasonable* bumping. Be careful of rainy days. You want to wrap the guitar in a plastic sheet before taking it outside in this case; the cover never does really clamp down tightly.

The padded carrying bag with its zipper closing usually offers lots of pockets and pouches for storing music, sandwiches and other extras (see below). A shoulder strap makes it ideal for trips when other luggage has to be schlepped along. It's fairly waterproof, but because of its soft construction, you should watch out for sharp corners.

The hardshell case is luggage-quality, with a padded inside (sometimes with a Leatherette exterior, clips, and locks) and is generally heavy but offers maximum protection. It's a must if your guitar is worth protecting. One of these can cost up to (and over) $100.

Extra Strings. Never get caught without extra strings. They always seem to break at the most unexpected and inopportune moments. With steel strings, the first (*E*) and second (*B*) strings are the most likely to go. Keep a full set and a few extra firsts and seconds around. With nylon strings, the fourth (*D*) wears out most often, because it is the thinnest of the wound strings. The first three (having no metal winding) never rust, and therefore they are more durable than the others. But like any other string, they can break, too.

Shoulder Strap. You may want to play standing up someday. Even when you are playing while sitting down, a shoulder strap can help you to balance the guitar and keep it from slipping and sliding around in your lap. The shoulder strap is tied around the peghead (not too close to the nut, or it will interfere with your left hand). The other end goes around the little *end pin*—like a buttonhole around a button. If your guitar has no end pin (many nylon-string guitars lack them), have your dealer put one on. A hole can be drilled and an end pin inserted in seconds.

Tuning Aids. A guitar pitch pipe is a set of six little whistles corresponding to the strings of the guitar. Some pitch pipes have only one whistle—usually tunes to *A* (440Hz)—the 5th fret of the first string. If a pitch pipe doesn't suit you, perhaps you might try a tuning fork, which is very accurate. The standard tuning fork is also *A*-440, and it is used as follows: Hold it by the stem, and tap the tines (the two vertical prongs—against a rubber heel or your knee. While it is vibrating, rest the tip of the stem against the bridge of the guitar. You will hear a pure, clear *A*.

One of the best answers to getting and staying in tune is the advent of low-cost electronic tuning meters. These devices allow you to electronically match the pitch of each string on a meter for extremely quick and accurate tuning.

Capo. This little device—there are several types—will be an invaluable aid, especially in the beginning of your studies. It will enable you to transpose songs into keys that will suit your voice before you have learned all the chords in other keys. Even after you have learned lots of chords, there will be situations where the judicious use of the capo will offer the best way out of a difficult situation.

Music Stand. Yes, a music stand! There is nothing worse than sitting on the edge of a bed, trying to keep the pages of a music book open while attempting to figure out a new chord, or strumming or singing an unfamiliar song. Make sure the music stand has some kind of device that will hold the pages flat. If you can't find one, clothespins will do just as well.

Picks. There are several different kinds of picks: flatpicks, thumbpicks and fingerpicks. You may not need them at the beginning of your studies.

Some people never use picks; some people always use them. Flatpicks are roughly triangular pieces of Celluloid, tortoiseshell, or plastic. They should be flexible enough so that they can move with equal ease up and down over the strings. A thumbpick fits over your right thumb (assuming you're right-handed) like a ring, between the nail and first joint. Fingerpicks fit similarly over your fingertips so as to aid either upward or downward movement.

Footstool. This is an optional piece of equipment. When playing seated, you may want to elevate one leg just a bit (this sometimes makes playing easier). Classical guitarists virtually always use footstools. Folk guitarists tend to drape themselves in a variety of positions—legs crossed, etc. For youngsters whose feet may dangle when seated on a chair of normal height, a footstool is a great stabilizing influence.

Peg Winder. Turning the tuning pegs may be hard on your fingers. Nylon strings have to be tightened and tightened and tightened before you can hear any pitch at all. A peg winder is a little gizmo that fits over the tuning peg and lets you rotate its handle in a more comfortable movement than endlessly turning the pegs between thumb and forefinger. You'll also find that the peg winder helps you get the job done much faster.

Humidifier. This is a little capsule that stays inside your case and keeps your guitar from drying out (and the wood from cracking). Not usually necessary unless you have a super delicate guitar and/or you live in Death Valley.

Jerry Silverman

2. STUDYING AND PRACTICING

Eddie Van Halen practicing.

WAYS TO PRACTICE

Before setting up a schedule we should really address ourselves to *when* to practice, *what* to practice, and *why* we are practicing. It seems many of us feel very despondent and discouraged because we don't get enough chance to woodshed. Then, when we do set aside some time, we just leap into it and quite often play the wrong things, things that form bad habits. But we're so grateful for the fact that we are finally working with guitar in hand, that we overlook what we're doing.

I've had quite a number of people tell me that, although they manage to practice several hours a day, they have this sinking lost feeling that their efforts are not doing them any good. Only you can best judge whether what you're working on is the right or wrong thing. Of course, the best thing would be to tackle weakness in your playing so that once those problems have been overcome they can help you realize more of your own goals. Those would be the things to consider. There's no point in continuing to focus on strengths during your practice period; this is like going to a gymnasium when you already have very large arms, and continuing to work on your arms, while your legs are thoroughly undeveloped because you never exercise them. What we want to do is focus on our strengths in public and eliminate our weaknesses in private.

Now some of these weaknesses may be in terms of the inability to grasp some concepts, theories, or styles of music. Also, there may be certain physical deficiencies, poor technique—not enough stretch in the left hand, no coordination between the two hands, an ineffective picking method. List what weaknesses you wish to overcome on a piece of paper. Then number them according to priorities and begin to work on them in this fashion, giving most immediate attention to the top item and so on. This is a good way of getting at *what* you should be practicing.

Before you begin to play any exercise, you should mentally ask yourself *why* you are playing that exercise. And the answer shouldn't be "because it's good for me"—that's too vague an answer—or "because my teacher told me to practice this." That doesn't tell you *why* he told you to practice it. You really should come up with an answer like: "The reason I'm practicing this particular drill is to strengthen the fourth finger of my left hand, because I haven't been using that finger and this exercise encourages its use." When you know exactly why you're working on any exercise, and then you further agree with yourself that you should indeed be working on it, it helps to motivate you to stick with the drill and play it more enthusiastically, thus obtaining better results.

There are many schools of thought on *when* you should practice and for *how long* and *how often*. Some people claim they never practice; they don't need it or they don't want it—they think it interferes. I can only go by results; in other words, if some musicians don't practice, and their playing is very good, and they're expanding musically, then it's right for them not to practice. For me, however, it seems to be something I want to do, and it seems like a good idea, so I do practice. In my estimation, it's a good idea to play every day. But the big thing to keep in mind is not how many hours per day, but *when was the last time in this day that the guitar was in your hands*. What I'm saying is, I think it's far better to play in several shorter periods during the day than to practice all at one stretch amounting to the same total number of hours. To me, 40 to 45 minutes is an ideal length for a practice session. After that time—since we are human organisms and subject to fatigue—the law of diminishing returns takes over, and we get less and less for our efforts. So after 45 minutes, it's a good idea to take a brief break, even for five minutes, before going on for another 45 minutes. This helps refresh your mind and your hands. Many players will purposely not take a break and will mistakenly tell themselves that they're so dedicated to their music that they cannot release themselves from it. But if you are dedicated, be dedicated enough to practice while fresh, not fatigued.

A good idea is to do something during the recess which is unrelated to what you've been doing for the past forty minutes. If you're sitting while playing, stand up; if possible, go outdoors, maybe stand under a tree where (because of photosynthesis) there's more oxygen; do some push-ups, splash some after-shave on your face—anything to change the routine you've been in.

Try to space your sessions through the day, so you don't go too long without playing a guitar, if this is at all possible and if you can coordinate it with your work and living schedules. For example, rather than practice every day between 10 in the morning and noon, try to divide it into three or four periods in the day so you practice a little in the morning, a little in the afternoon, and some in the evening. Ideally, the time between sessions shouldn't be more than four hours. If you play from 10 to noon, that's good, but consider that it will be 22 hours before you pick up a guitar again. For anyone who's very serious about growing on the guitar, it is not in your best interests to be away from the instrument for that long.

Try to set up your practice periods so that part of the time is spent on things that will lead to physical growth—that is, things that will strengthen or coordinate your hands—and part of the time concentrate on theoretical problems, learning how to write or arrange, breaking down syncopated time patterns. Divide your time and efforts between physical skills and mental concepts of music. (When practicing how to read syncopated lines, incidentally, it's good to have someone check your accuracy and give you feedback. There are many other things you can practice—a scale, a song—and you know yourself that you're playing them the right way. But this is one kind of study where if you're not really sure, there's no way to know if you're playing correctly or not, so you do need somebody who knows syncopation to observe and check.)

When playing an exercise, I believe it's very important to learn about the drill and everything connected with it. You should do this very slowly and deliberately at first, noting all the points that are necessary. I cannot emphasize enough the importance of playing exercises slowly. As time goes on, and as you repeat the example, it will become more habitual, more automatic, and the speed will then increase as a result of the constant repetition. Slowly grasp intellectually what it is you're going to do; later the necessary skills will begin to develop, and your speed and smoothness will increase. Don't get impatient; don't rush into something feeling that you have to do it very fast from the outset.

Once a particular drill has found its way from your "intellectual center" to your "moving center" it should stay there and continue to get more solidified. At that point it would be best not to move the new skill back to your intellectual center, since it can never play the exercise as fast or as well as the moving center.

Practice certain things both with and without a metronome. When practicing with the metronome, you're using it as your drummer, to keep time. Control the speed at which you're going to play the exercise and increase the tempo gradually as your proficiency improves. Also, every few months you should change the material you're working with—not the factors you need to improve, but the means by which you're grooming your skills.

Barney Kessel

SELF-INSTRUCTION

One of the most difficult and ungroovy things about playing the guitar, and especially *learning* how to play guitar, is practicing. The image of a child practicing the piano on a sunny day while the others were out playing baseball is shared by many folks I know, myself included. There are a few dedicated souls who practice several hours a day, and there is no doubt that their technique improves substantially as a result. There is also a lot to be said for formal instruction. A good teacher can show you things in a span of a few months that would take you years to figure out on your own. But most people never really take advantage of one of the best teachers available: oneself.

Training, practicing scales, learning music theory—all these things are important to a guitar player, just as understanding brush techniques and the ability to mix the right paints to obtain the desired hues and textures are to a painter. But all the same paints and brushes are available to every musician. One might deduce from this data that all painters therefore paint alike and all musicians play the same way. Of course, they don't. There are elements which are unique to everyone's playing, painting, or whatever. What quality, then, is it that the artist possesses which makes for this "uniqueness factor"? I would propose that a great deal of it has to do with how the individual musician relates to all the music he or she has heard during their lifetime. And not only does the individual relate to this backlog of music in its entirety, but also in specific ways according to specific times of their life.

There is no doubt that certain *rhythms* are the common denominator for quite a few people, as evidenced by the heartbeat music called disco. The heartbeat common denominator even extends to the time we spent in the womb. But *melody* can be much more of a common denominator than most people realize. For instance, we are all familiar with religious music in some way or another. If the scorer of a movie soundtrack wanted to give a religious or church-like flavor to a particular scene, he might write a melody that, even though it may not have been drawn from a particular hymn, nevertheless contains elements that would bring to mind a "church-ish" image. The ability of the artist to further render his or her image believable is then a function of technical ability and an overall grasp of theory.

What does all this have to do with self instruction? Very simply, everyone relates to music differently, has different "favorite tunes," etc. But many of these relationships are shared by quite a few people. For example, one thing which many people can relate to is the comedy team of Laurel & Hardy. If, in a particular moment during a solo, you wished to convey a sense of comedy to the general musical statement, not only might you play a melody using bits of slapstick comedy music, but you might even quote the Laurel & Hardy theme in a quick 2-bar phrase.

This is where the self-instruction comes in. It is easy to use that major scale theme in a major key, say *G* major. But what if the changes you are soloing over are in a minor key, like *E* minor? How do you use your little idea? Well, you might know (a little theory necessary here) that *G* major is the relative major of *E* minor. So if you played the theme in *G* major it would indeed fit. You might even take it so far as to play a flat 3rd (the third note of the *G* major scale would be *B*) which would allow you to play the melody with a minor key feeling, making it possible to convey not only a very explicit image, but also to use this image in a melancholy piece of music which was probably written in a minor key intentionally to take advantage of the melancholy feeling a minor key can evoke from most people.

From then on, it can become as sophisticated as what you can think up and play. These melodies are like your own private music books and lessons. Play them backwards, forwards, lower the 3rd, raise the 5th, practice your lessons as much and with as much variety as you want. Tired of comedy themes? Try nursery rhymes. They convey an entirely separate set of images and emotions, as well as offering new lessons.

I believe that melody is the lyric of dreams and emotions, and using these melodies from your own experience will allow you not only to say what you want with greater subtlety, but also to strengthen any lyric that might happen to be a part of a song you're working on. By the way, one of my favorites is the first four bars of "Catch A Falling Star" by Perry Como.

Jeff Baxter

THE VALUE OF SCALES

Based on my own personal experiences, it seems to me that most musicians in all walks of life either give far too much or far too little time and attention to the playing of musical scales. For me, scales are not music, but a means for making music. They are predictable, orderly, and sequential, but do not contain the life force found in a strong melodic statement.

Playing scales helps an instrumentalist gain technique and become familiar with the "territory" of the tonal center of the key he happens to be in at the moment. For example, look at this harmonic pattern:

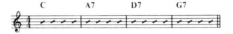

With a thorough knowledge of the scales of the four chords, you could not only play the melody and its variations but also move through this with ease and really get into what the harmonic progression is all about; instead of "fishing" for a few random notes that might fit without clashing with each chord.

While this familiarity with scales is desirable and commendable, it is merely *preparing* to make music, and falls short of good melodic and rhythmic inventiveness. To use an analogy, each musical tone is like a letter of the alphabet. A scale is like a group of letters arranged alphabetically, and a brief melodic string of perhaps one or two measures is like a word. A melodic statement of perhaps four to eight measures is like a sentence, therefore an entire song of perhaps 32 measures is like a paragraph. An arrangement of the song with an introduction, interlude(s), and coda is like a short story or article. A production version of this song in which the length of performance time is increased, with perhaps singing and/or dancing segments with a vocal chorus or elaborate choreography, is similar to a book. A symphony based on the thematic materlal is like a large literary work. The purpose of this analogy is to show what position scales occupy in the hierarchy of musical values.

In my opinion, the use of scales in improvisation does not contribute much musical value—except as an effect or color that may be desired at the moment. There is neither spontaneity nor creativity in playing a scale while improvising; there is no musical statement in a scale. Since it is a predetermined succession of sequentially-arranged tones it is, in a sense, no different than a "lick," or a "run," or an arpeggio, or any musical fragment or device built upon a formula. A scale is preset; void of the living, emotional, and dynamic elements which are produced through spontaneity, creativity, imagination, and instantaneous experimentation. A scale is a musical treadmill—it keeps moving, but it doesn't go anywhere.

One should not reduce a song down to its harmonic content and then reduce it further down to a set of scales based on the harmonic structure, because in doing so, one limits possibilities during improvisation. Void of the rhythmic, melodic, and harmonic textures inherent in the material, all songs become a series of scales. It is like looking at a person and seeing a numerical equation instead of a human force simultaneously possessing personality, intelligence, character, and ability. How depersonalized can you get?

Scales are, in a way, musically depersonalized textures, void of the elements that form the basis for good music. In conclusion, it is of great benefit (it can't hurt) for every musician to know the theory behind building scales and to know how to play them on his instrument. These two capabilities will help the guitarist improve his or her technique on the instrument and solidify familiarity with the entire musical area surrounding the tonal center. Playing scales is preparing to make music; it is not music. In improvising, when one decides to play a scale, the decision must be spontaneous. Without proper training, however, the execution of the scale may not be.

Playing scales is like a boxer punching a bag, skipping rope, and sparring with a partner. Making music—employing scales and all of the other possibilities—is like the main event of a boxing exhibition.

Scales have nothing to do with jazz, improvisation, self-expression, the emotional qualities in music, or the type of playing that draws from the essence of the soul. That is why, in my opinion, it is wise not to ignore scales nor to project more importance on them than they deserve, but (like all other elements in music) to use them only when the music dictates that their use would be appropriate.

Barney Kessel

HAND EXERCISES OF THE PROS

A guitarist speaks through his hands. Eloquence is achieved by coordinating the miraculous network of ligaments, tendons, nerves, metacarpals, and phalanges that lie encased at the end of each arm in gloves of flesh. Coordination is easier pronounced than obtained, since the natural tendency of hands is to *not* play the guitar. So how does a flamenco guitarist refine the mundane action of drumming a table in boredom into the elegant purr of a *rasgueado*? And how does the classical musician get a muscle (the lumbricalis) about the size and shape of one Kraft macaroni noodle firmed up enough to bulge its way through two minutes of barre chords for Sor's "Etude #19 in B♭?" And how does the jazz, rock, folk, or blues instrumentalist keep a blaze of sixty-fourth notes clear and distinct when one hand's fingers are blindly hurdling frets and trying to land precisely as the pick snaps like blue sparks from string to string? The problem is definitely two-fisted.

An end to this hand to hand combat is achieved by the *simultaneous* development of strength, suppleness, and limberness. And this is primarily a result of exercise of one sort of another. For those who shudder at the very word, remember that "exercise" is used loosely here. We're merely examining the phenomenon to which, consciously or unconsciously, nearly all guitarists devote some (however small) portion of their playing time. They run through little warmups (if nothing other than a familiar lick) to wake up their fingers, rid their joints of creaks and pops ,and get both hands moving together so that music rather than amusement will be the result when the "serious" playing begins. The amount of time spent "exercising" and the degree of complexity of favorite "etudes" may vary from person to person, but in fact a comparison of the most bizarre contortions with the most simpleminded diddling reveals that neither is as apparently impossible or useless as superficial analysis might at first indicate.

Really only two categories of "exercises" exist. Those done with the guitar in hands, and those done without the guitar. Perhaps the most popular method of hand development while holding the guitar is the execution of scales, arpeggios, tremolos, and the like. Juan Serrano, the flamenco virtuoso, dedicates one hour a day to *each* technique before he plays anything else. Jazz greats Jerry Hahn and Joe Pass follow the same course (though not necessarily for as long). Pass advises that guitarists first practice slowly and evenly (then faster) all forms of a scale—in thirds and fourths, etc.—major, minor, augmented, diminished, dominant-seventh, modal, chromatic. "It is important," he says, "to go slowly, moderately, and to be absolutely sure that *every note* is clear and definite. Then progressively go faster, ending as fast and clean as you can, and do this at least one hour a day."

Precision can also be developed on the fingerboard with open tunings in folk-oriented Robbie Basho's manner: "In a *C* tuning, *C, G, C, G, C, E* [6th-1st string]," he states, "I play the open string, 2nd fret, 4th fret, and 5th fret on each string using thumb, first finger, third finger, and little finger respectively up the scale, utilizing different rhythm patterns such as 1 2 3 4, 5 6 7 8, or 1 2 3, 4 5 6, or 1 2 3 4, 2 2 3 4."

Fingerstyle great Chet Atkins stretches his left hand fingers by practicing chords that extend beyond three or four frets. He also feels that the best way to strengthen the hands is to practice on a guitar that had a stiff or high action that makes it hard to play. "You build muscles," he elaborates. "and it thickens the calluses on the left hand. After playing on a stiff, high-action guitar, I can play my good guitar with more confidence and dexterity."

Les Paul disagrees. "I believe in practicing on the same instrument I will use in performing," he says. "And with electric," he adds, "I have the speaker facing me while I practice to be certain I'm not fooling myself." Les, among others, is somewhat looser in his approach to "exercise." The only hand exercise he uses is playing. He avoids getting trapped into one method of playing by picking the same arpeggio, scale, run, lick, or whatever in several different ways (all down, while pulling or hammering strings, etc.), varying his picking stroke and angle. "Up and down strokes may give me a clear, even run," he explains, "but it may also sound mechanical. Practicing and combining the various methods of fingering and picking is bound to help in coordinating the mind and fingers. And lots of practice is going to give the necessary speed and strength. The amount of practice time needed will vary between players, but who watches the clock when you love the instrument?"

Herb Ellis echoes this relaxed approach. "Just to get my hands limber," he states, "I slowly play a tune with a lot of chords; then I play a few choruses of blues or some other tune very fast. All this doesn't take long and I am now ready to play or practice." A younger voice from the jazz world, Phil Upchurch, reiterates Herb's and Les' view. Phil relies entirely on regular daily practice with extra attention given to the phrases that give him the most trouble. "I think ball squeezing and the like is for the birds," Upchurch says.

Phil's comment introduces the issue of exercises *away* from the guitar, and Barney Kessel would have to include himself among "the birds." At times, he's found that it's possible to strengthen his hands and fingers through squeezing exercises. He uses "a little rubber ball—a very small one, the kind little girls use to play jacks with." Wilburn Burchette, a guitarist and inventor of the Impro guitar, also uses a rubber ball, though a larger one: A hand ball two inches in diameter. "I use the ball," he says, "like a stick of chewing gum. I always have one with me, and whenever I find my hands are free, I let my fingers 'chew' the ball. Just like chewing gum, I find it to be a very relaxing and effortless habit. It's a very easy way to develop and maintain great hand strength, limberness, and dexterity."

Laurindo Almeida, who fuses Brazilian and classical styles, doesn't bother with a rubber ball and simply does hand clenches. While lying down in bed before going to sleep he opens and closes his fingers of both hands five hundred times ordinarily and a thousand times on days preceding concerts. "It really keeps my tendons soft and flexible," he says, though he's quick to caution against violent or strenous exercises which can damage the hands.

The question arises whether strength per se is even particularly relevant to good guitaring. Howard Roberts and classical guitarist Michael Lorimer emphasize the ability to relax more than clutch or grasp. Roberts concedes that "Isometrics can be a real time saver, but strength is only part of the picture. The ability to apply pressure and suddenly relax—on, off, on, off—is the big deal." Lorimer concurs, for he does not view the guitar as an instrument which demands physical strength at all. In his opinion, playing well is more a matter of balance, coordination, and feel; and only when one has not balanced one's hand correctly does it seem as if strength is required. Lorimer's method of assuring hand balance is to find the easiest position to hold a fist and then to relax the fingers so that the thumb is centered opposing the left hand fingers. Assuming the arm and hand are relaxed, the left hand technique should be the same when the right hand is similarly centered). The strokes should be *very* quick and short. "Just *release* the string, don't attack it, and relax the fingers that are not playing. The important matter is coordination between mind—what I hear inside—and body—what I hear outside and so with my hands. Practice for me consists of *realizing* what I hear inside."

Somewhat more unorthodox exercises would include the type Kessel has mentioned in his column: magic tricks. "As a pastime," he related, "I shuffle cards, and do little card tricks, and magic tricks—making cards disappear, this kind of thing—for little kids (and a few adults along the way) who don't know what I am doing. In manipulating the cards it does increase my finger ability. This flexibility has stayed in my fingers, and I suppose I use it on the guitar."

Lorimer says that some of his students have found the following exercise to be useful for relaxing and stretching the left hand: Sit in a chair and straighten your left leg. Form a "V" by spreading any two fingers and put the "V" over the top of the knee cap (palm on your thigh). Now slowly bend the leg and feel the stretching in your fingers.

A final word from Laurindo Almeida: "Robert Schumann, the German composer of the Romantic Era, began to experiment on his own with a mechanical device for finger-strengthening which disabled one of the fingers of his right hand. In fact, this was the accident that terminated his last hopes of a career as a virtuoso, and he *never* fully regained the use of his right hand. One should be careful of, or better yet—stay away from, mechanical devices in order to avoid accidents."

We are not necessarily recommending any of these "exercises." We are merely presenting a sampling that some musicians have found to be helpful in their own development. Like any other instrument, the hand can be permanently damaged if mistreated. Barney Kessel has always warned against practicing too long, and advises guitarists to avoid muscular strain and fatigue. He feels that four fifteen-minute practice sessions a day are often more beneficial than one uninterrupted hour.

The philosophy that one isn't getting something out of an exercise unless it hurts is like recommending that the best way to toughen the skin is to cut it until it bleeds. Pain and fatigue are messages signalling abuse or impending abuse, not "progress." In particular, if one has an already existent physical disability in the hands, it would be wise to consult a doctor and get a diagnosis to find out if any if any of the hand exercises we've mentioned would in fact be detrimental to the particular condition.

Don Menn

PHILOSOPHY AND FUNDAMENTALS OF GOOD TECHNIQUE

Just for a second, let's accept the premise that there's no such thing as the "right way" to do things, and whatever gets results is kosher. As examples of the success of this approach, you might cite Pete Townshend's or Wes Montgomery's use of the left-hand thumb for chording. You could also point to Jimmy Page's ultra-low-slung Les Paul, Django Reinhardt's partially crippled but virtuosic left hand, or Jimi Hendrix' upside-down, backward guitar position. An unorthodox approach to technique never prevented any of these guitarists from earning legendary status.

Okay, sure, *but* (a great, big, wide "but"), these are all artists—gifted individuals. Perhaps they grew into strange habits and styles because they never knew any better; in some cases they were driven by that mother of invention, necessity. But you, gentle Back to Basics reader, are (assumedly) just beginning your musical quest in a marvelous, modern media and telecommunications era—there's no reason for *you* to be uninformed, no reason why *you* should have to make up techniques as you go. So know thy place, and heed the master's highly available voice. Your time will come—for now, let experience talk to you with the wisdom of pure, unadulterated common sense, which is the voice of *good technique*.

Example: Teacher says, "Keep your left-hand thumb low, centered in the middle-back of the neck, while you finger the strings with a straight-down, tip-of-the-finger approach. Keep the wrist down and forward, the hand bent up and in." (See Figure 1 and Figure 2.)

Pupil says, "Aaugh! Why? It's damned uncomfortable, and I can't finger the strings as easily as when I let my thumb slide up and I squeeze the neck like a baseball bat." (See Figure 3 and Figure 4.]

Now the teacher explains with infinite patience and the wisdom of experience that indeed it's true—the thumb-high, left-hand squeeze approach is unrivaled for strength, and when playing leads and bending strings, the thumb *should* swivel up higher for more stability. But the vast majority of playing is not string-bending leads: Scale runs, arpeggios, chords, barres, and wide-reaching intervals requiring the stretch of the pinky are all greatly facilitated by the hand position shown in Figure 1 and Figure 2, and severely hampered by the positions shown in Figure 3 and Figure 4.

So, here in the class of basics, one must learn not to take shortcuts just to produce results. Why? Because (pay attention, now—this is the moral of the story) the traditional, fundamental aspects of physical technique can be expanded on infinitely, but shortcuts taken at *this* stage can become bad habits not easily broken, often leading to dead ends. Every learning step you take now has far-reaching consequences in your playing later. Why limit your options?

Learn to sit before you stand, and walk before you run: Rock stars may jump around the stage with their guitars dangling down around their kneecaps and look cool, but let us consider some basic techniques first, shall we? Even when you are sitting, a strap is a good idea—it keeps the neck positioned well in relation to your upper body, prevents the guitar from wandering around on your lap, and allows you to simply play the instrument without being concerned with holding and supporting its weight.

As far as technique goes (and I don't necessarily believe it's the be-all and end-all of guitar playing), I think you should envision classical guitar technique, and then modify it to apply to acoustic or electric playing, whether pickstyle or not. Classical technique is traditional, time-tested, and true. Centuries of examination and refinement have made it the technical art closest to perfection, so if you're going to develop your own style, habits, and techniques (which is inevitable if you hang in long

Figure 1.

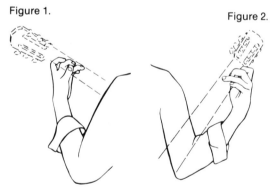

Figure 2.

Figure 3.

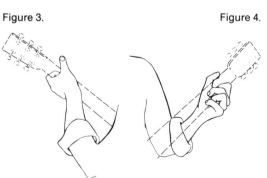

Figure 4.

enough), it certainly won't do you any harm to start out from the most logical, commonsense base: the classical approach.

Now that you're holding the instrument correctly, let's play it! Look at the G major chord shown in Example 1. A lot of players finger it with the 1st, 2nd, and 3rd fingers, but I recommend getting used to using the pinky (as shown) for reasons stated earlier: utilizing your full potential. Besides, using the 3rd, 2nd, and 4th fingers for G makes possible all the interesting variations shown in Examples 2-5. Have fun.

Rik Emmett

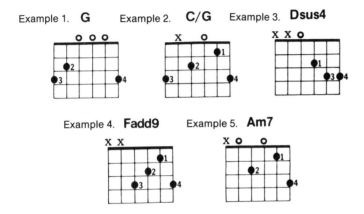

Example 1. **G**   Example 2. **C/G**   Example 3. **Dsus4**

Example 4. **Fadd9**   Example 5. **Am7**

RECOMMENDED ALBUMS
FOR THE DEVELOPING GUITARIST

Sitting before a phonograph with instrument in hand and lifting licks, chords, and inspiration off of black vinyl discs is for a guitarist a tradition as common as carving a turkey on Thanksgiving or raising the flag on the Fourth of July. Countless pickers, young and old, have been doing it since the days when the record player had a crank on its side and a large, fluted horn attached to the tonearm. Since the day in 1877 when its inventor, Thomas Edison, first uttered, "Mary had a little lamb" into a crude "talking machine," the phonograph has been a huge success as a learning apparatus. Its most obvious advantage is its handiness: If you want to hear Charlie Christian or Django Reinhardt, you simply place a record on the turntable and you're already to roll.

Naturally, some purists are dead set against the very idea of learning by simply listening to records; to some, anything short of learning to read written notation is heresy, and not worthy of serious consideration. Almost no one, though, can deny that listening to music is a great way to sharpen your ear.

While some guitarists have learned almost exclusively by listening to records, others with formal musical training have turned to discs as an aid to the rapid learning of songs, particularly those not published in sheet music. And no matter how well you read music, you may often find that accurate transcriptions of guitar solos are difficult to find; in fact, chords are almost invariably oversimplified, giving a misleading picture of the harmonic structure. And even if the notes are correct, how do you precisely notate nuances such as tone, vibrato technique, or the timbral coloration of effects? Just listening to a record can tell you an awful lot.

Some of *Guitar Player*'s Advisory Board members have suggested the artists and records that they feel would be beneficial to guitarists interested in picking up stylistic pointers from recorded sources. In some cases, genres of music or specific artists have been mentioned, rather than particular albums or songs. You can often find records that showcase various styles of works by these musicians in the form of anthologies (e.g., the *Cruisin'* series from the late '50s and early '60s).

Of course, some of the records may be difficult to locate for a variety of reasons—the record companies are obscure, the records were pressed in small quantities, or they're out of print—but none are *impossible* to find. Check your local record store. They probably have either a *Schwann Guide* or a large, yellow book called the *Phonolog*. Both are updated periodically, and include thousands of records currently stocked. They don't list many obscure labels, however.

Bargain bins at record, drug, and department stores are good (and often inexpensive) sources for some of the true gems. For the real searchers, there are attics, basements, flea markets, and garage sales. Also, in some towns there are stores devoted soley to oldies or collector's records. Check want ads in music publications, as well as record auction newsletters. Some public libraries stock records and tapes; inquire at the main desk.

Diligence will often pay off; you may even run across a goldmine of fantastic records that you weren't aware of. Just getting the word out to friends and relatives may bring excellent results. You might be surprised to find that someone you have known for years is an avid collector, or a fan of the very person whose records you are seeking.

Doc Watson. Most of the people I listened to when I was learning to play guitar weren't solo guitarists; they were primarily accompanists. There was some picking, but most of it was there to back up the singing. Great players in this category were Jimmie Rodgers, the original Carter Family, the Delmore Brothers, and Merle Travis. For basic country licks, the Delmore Brothers are good to listen to because their music is so down-to-earth, and nothing fancy. For real virtuoso fingerpicking, there's no one better than Chet Atkins. Just about anything by the original Carter Family is excellent for more basic things. I learned my beginning licks by listening to Maybelle Carter, and my basic strums from Jimmie Rodgers. Picking up fiddle licks is often more difficult, but Kenny Baker, Joe Green, Tommy Jackson, and Paul Warren albums are good if you want to learn some challenging lines. And although they can be difficult to transpose to guitar, Bill Monroe's bluegrass mandolin songs are really good. For some less easier, involved mandolin lines, listen to Bill and Earl Bullock of the Blues Cowboys.

Johnny Smith. Although I can't suggest any specific albums, I think a good place to begin is by listening to music from the swing era—in particular material by Django Reinhardt and Charlie Christian. Another great from that period was George Barnes, who was a hard-driving player who used mostly down-stroke picking—probably a throwback to the days before amps were used, and it was a necessity for jazz guitarists to develop a strong picking hand in order to be heard over the other instruments in the band. George Van Eps used terrific harmonized chord lines, too. Tony Mottola is a really great studio player who did a lot of recording in the early days of television. He was certainly one of the pioneers of electric guitar in the studio, and one of the finest sight-readers.

In the progressive jazz vein, listen to Jimmy Raney's work with Stan Getz. Tal Farlow's work with [vibraphonist] Red Norvo's trio is a good example of fantastic technique. Herb Ellis's playing in the early '50s and Chuck Wayne's when he was a member of the George Shearing Quintet were marvelous. Other greats to listen to are Barney Kessel, Joe Pass, and Lenny Breau. A fine guitarist from Dublin, Ireland, is Louis Stewart. Of course, all of Chet Atkin's music is great. Also, I think that guitarists should listen to other types of instrumentalists in order to learn different phrasing, melodic, and tonal techniques. Pianist Art Tatum was a fantastic technician, and saxophonists Charlie Parker and Stan Getz have an awful lot to offer.

Tal Farlow. I think it's important for all guitarists to go back and listen to anything they can get by Charlie Christian, Django Reinhardt, George Van Eps, Barney Kessel, Jim Hall, Johnny Smith, George Barnes, Wes Montgomery, and Jimmy Raney. Charlie Christian and all the big band guitarists had a big effect on me. Albums by non-guitarists such as tenor saxophonist Lester Young, alto saxophonist Charlie Parker, and pianists Art Tatum and Bud Powell are good sources for interesting lines. A real challenge is transcribing piano music for guitar. Whereas you only use one hand's fingers on the guitar, all ten are in use on the piano. Listen to guitarists Bucky Pizzarelli, Lenny Breau, Pat Martino, and John McLaughlin. And if something appeals to you, don't be afraid to copy from it; don't worry about being called a copycat. Worry about that *after* you can play many different licks. You need to have reference points.

Larry Coryell. Keyboardist Les McCann's *Somethin' Special* features Joe Pass on guitar, Groove Holmes on organ, and Joe Splink on sax. It's a great representation of Pass's responding to the musicians around him. His timing is swinging and precise. McCann and Holmes were terrific as a keyboard duo. Kenny Burrell's guitar work on *Midnight Blue* [Blue Note, 84123], and particularly the song "Chit'lins Con Carne," is mellow, but full of fire. Kenny's solo shows sophistication while being funky, and that he understands how to use the minor 7th #9th chord, as well as the blues cadences normally associated with rock and roll. There's no piano on the record, so you can hear how he holds down the harmonies. Also, listen to *Kenny Burrell Live At The Five Spot.*

In the late '50s Barney Kessel has three volumes of 10" records that I found really inspirational—his ballads, open bass strings, and melodic solos are very strong, lyrical, and emotional, like a great horn player's. Tal Farlow's work on *Red Norvo With Strings* [re-released as part of *Guitar Player*, Prestige, 24042] also transcended the basic guitar idiom. His playing is delicate but exciting, and the arrangements throughout are amazing. *Movin'* [Milestone, M-47040] is a reissue of two of Wes Montgomery's great jazz albums. On *Movin' Along*, the first of the two albums, Wes's playing throughout is superb. His use of octaves is noteworthy, too. Wes told me that the second album in the reissue, *Full House*, was his favorite album at the time of its release in 1960. On it was [trumpeter] Miles Davis's rhythm section, and the entire album was recorded live. Johnny Smith's early-'50s LP, *In A Mellow Mood*, is great for mellowing down late at night. Smith's style of chording is unusual in that he uses so many close chord voicings; he makes them all sound deceptively easy, but they're killers to play. His soloing, syncopation, and everything else are great. Jim Hall's chordal guitar playing on saxophonist Paul Desmond's *Bossa Antiqua* is absolutely unbelievable. He also shows that you don't have to be flashy all the time to be great. His playing on flugelhornist Art Farmer's *Live At The Half Note* is also stunning. *Return To Forever* [ECM, 1022] is one of the best jazz-fusion style albums of its kind. It is also one of the last albums that Bill Connors played electric guitar on extensively. Chick Corea and Stanley Clarke made the album extra good. In the blues vein, Albert King's solo on "Crosscut Saw" from *Born Under A Bad Sign* [Stax, S723] says it all. He's got such taste, fine dynamics, and just plain great musicianship.

Juan Serrano. Ramon Montoya is considered by many to be the father of modern flamenco. He pioneered new techniques and harmonizations in the idiom, and his music inspired most of today's flamenco players. A good example of his work is *Arte Clasico Flamenco* [Philharmonia (17 E. 48th St. New York, NY 10019), PH 108]. A modern type of flamenco with a jazz influence is Paco de Lucia's *Fuente Y Caudal* [Philips Avda De America Sin, Madrid, Spain), 63 28 109]. And around 1950 Perico El Del

Lunar's *Antologia Flamenco* was recorded in France; it won several awards in Europe, and it breathed new life into the art that was declining in popularity. *Flamenco Puro* by Sabicas is a good study in syncopations in use today. My album, *Ole La Mano* [Elektra, EKS 7227] is a good example of flamenco in its pure, traditional form.

Stanley Clarke. I think that Jimi Hendrix's *Are You Experienced?* [Reprise 6261] was a good example of a totally new concept in music. Noel Redding's bass playing was perfect for the music and Jimi's guitar playing is fantastic. I think Larry Graham's *Graham Central Station* [Warner Bros., B-2763] is the best funk album to date. His bass playing fills the bill perfectly. And his work on *Stand!* [Epic, 26456] with Sly And The Family Stone is a great example of his ability to work in an ensemble. Jaco Pastorius's solo album, *Jaco Pastorius* [Epic, PE 33949], is an excellent example of fretless bass playing. Every cut on the album is good, and keyboardist Herbie Hancock and drummer Lenny White are also great on it. For modern jazz, Miroslav Vitous's *Infinite Search* [Atlantic, SD 1622] showcases a lot of great acoustic bass work that covers the whole range of sounds, including a tone much like an electric. A landmark of progressive rock from the late '60s is *Fresh Cream* [RSO, RS-1-3009]; Jack Bruce's bass lines and Eric Clapton's guitar work have a good blues feel. Stevie Wonder's *Night On The Town* [Motown, out of print] features really nice grooves—it's a good example of rhythm and blues. My *Stanley Clarke* [Nemporer, NE 431], *Journey To Love* [Nemporer, NE 433], and *School Days* [Nemporer, NE 439] all contain good examples of complex bass lines, finger popping style, and well-recorded acoustic bass. A real killer to play is "Life Is Just A Game" [from *School Days*], but the song "School Days" is a natural for the electric bass.

Jeff Baxter. Two albums that I got while I was really young were by Howard Roberts: *Color Him Funky* [Capitol, ST-1887] and *H.R. Is A Dirty Guitar Player* [Capitol, SM-1961]. They are full of really fine, clean guitar playing that has a blues base to it. There is just enough jamming on them to grab guitarists and let them concentrate on the playing, and the format is very accessible. Most beginning guitarist, I feel, are interested in blues and rock and roll patterns, and because of their similarities in many respects, it's easy to get into these records. Another great album is the Ventures' *Walk Don't Run* [Liberty (dist. by United Artists), 8003], which is, in a sense, like a recorded exercise book. The formats of all the songs are very similar, so in essence you are able to go through the tunes and learn the licks as if they were variations on a basic theme. Listening to their music can also help you develop a very steady sense of rhythm—upstrokes, down-strokes, etc. Any and all "greatest hits" albums from the 1950s and '60s are terrific for getting a background in rock and roll. They're like a set of encyclopedias for getting you into the basic style. A lot of young guitarists aren't in tune with the roots of rock and roll—they hear people covering old Buddy Holly and Chuck Berry tunes for instance—and think that they're hearing the original because they aren't aware. There's a whole legacy of rock and roll from the '50s and '60s to learn from.

compiled by Tom Mulhern

G

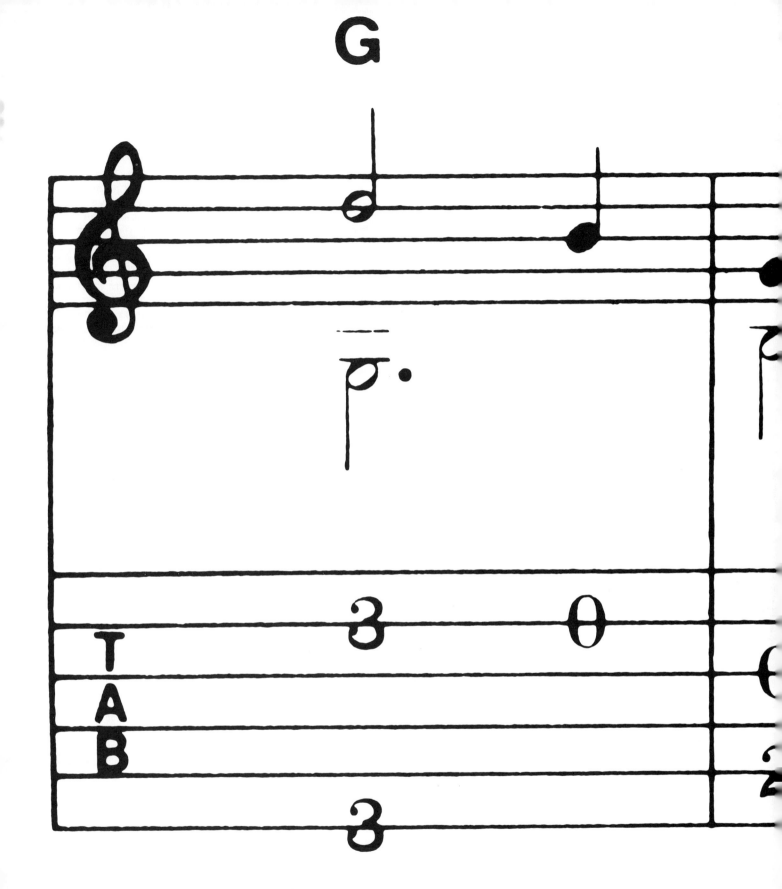

3. READING

THE NECESSITY OF READING MUSIC

Most of you who read *Guitar Player* are probably aware of the fact that guitarists (regardless of style) have the reputation of not being able to read music, or at least the reputation for being poor readers. This attitude has slightly changed in the past decade, but not enough to convince many musicians that the guitarist should be allowed to sit in with a symphony orchestra. Although this article will not involve any musical examples, it will suggest some very practical ways in which to improve your reading skills.

First, I think we should list several guitar styles and show the level of reading ability among guitarists in each genre. This analysis is based on my 20 years of experience in crossing all types of guitar players, and by no means is the final word (there are plenty of exceptions); however, trust me that the general assumptions are accurate. The list starts with the best guitar readers and ends with the worst, and takes into account the overall ability to read music, knowledge of the fingerboard, sight-reading facility, horizontal reading (single notes), and vertical reading (notes stacked upon one another—chords, counterpoint, etc).

1. Studio
2. Jazz
3. Classical
4. Rock
5. Pop
6. Country
7. Blues
8. Flamenco
9. Folk

It's not hard to guess that studio guitarists would be the best readers. They have usually spent the most time practicing their reading in preparation for becoming session players. In general, jazz guitarists have also spent a great deal of time with written music, and in many cases have attended universities that stress the reading of music. Classical guitarists usually spend a large amount of time in learning to read music; their goal is usually to learn how to read well enough in order to read or transcribe classical guitar compositions and then memorize them. Unfortunately, classical guitarists are usually poor sight-readers.

Starting with the rock, pop, and country guitarists, the levels of reading drop considerably for a few simple reasons. In the case of the rock guitarist, he or she usually starts to pick up the guitar by ear. This is by no means a detriment; in fact, I've noticed that many rock and pop guitarists have better ear training than the studio, jazz, or classical players. As we know, some of the most innovative guitar playing has come from rock guitarists who did not read a note (e.g. Jimi Hendrix). So if you plan to be in that category, you need not read further. However, for those of you who are a little more practical, you can see that the days of the rock guitarist not needing to read music are over. There are just too many guitarists out there competing for the same job.

The blues, flamenco, and folk guitarsits are usually the worst readers, but I don't mean any insult. The traditions for learning such styles run very deep, and in the past have had very little to do with reading written music.

Looking at this list of guitar stylists and their general reading abilities, you might get some idea of where you fit in. For example, if you are a folk guitarist looking to break into the studios, you just may have a great deal of work cut out for yourself in the reading department.

There are several steps you can take right away to help improve your reading. First of all, give yourself this test to determine your weakest points:

1. Randomly select a note, such as *B*♭. Play it on each string, starting with the sixth up to the first, as fast as you can. For example, if you were using the note *B*♭, you would go from the sixth string's 6th fret to the fifth string's 1st fret, the fourth string's 8th fret, the third string's 3rd fret, the second string's 11th fret, and the first string's 6th fret. If you can complete the test from the sixth string to the first

string in between one and two second's time, you have an excellent knowledge of the fingerboard. Three to four seconds is average; if it takes longer than that—well, you know you need some work. Try this exercise with all the chromatic tones.

2. Write down on music paper as many random notes as you can think of. Use natural notes, sharps, flats, and notes way above and below the staff. Make sure you assign *no* rhythmic value to the notes, Read these notes on the guitar as fast as you can. Then put down the guitar and merely recite them, including all flats, naturals, and sharps (for example, *A, F♯, B♮, D,* etc). If you were able to recite the notes quickly, then your basic knowledge of the staff, ledger lines, etc. is probably adequate. If you slowed down when you played the same notes on the instrument, your knowledge of the fingerboard is possibly weak. If you did well *playing* the notes on your guitar but slowed down considerably when you recited them, then your basic understanding of the notes on the staff is probably weak. By the way, this test should include both treble and bass clefs; I believe it helps *greatly* for a guitarist to be able to read in both clefs.

3. This part of the test involves writing out a rhythmic pattern with no pitch content (for example: ♪♩ ♪♫). Copy the rhythmic values for a piece of music, or make your own. Next, either sing or tap out the rhythm and see how your performance compares to parts 1 and 2 of the test. If you have an easy time with them, but you're having trouble tapping out the correct rhythm of part 3, then you'll know the weakest part of your reading ability and you can concentrate on improving it.

Be honest with yourself, and if you really can't accurately pinpoint what part you're weak in, try the tests with a friend or a teacher. If you're weak in all three areas, really get to work!

Currently in the United States (and probably abroad) there are more guitarists earning a living professionally than ever before. The competitiveness is incredible, and if you don't know how to read music your chances of making it will become less and less real. The 1960s witnessed an incredible boom in rock music and many people took up the guitar. The children of the '60s are coming out in droves, and a whole lot of them are monster guitar players!

If I could give any advice to young guitar players, it would be simply two things: Learn to read music, and study ear training. If you can hear a piece of music and play it immediately, and also read music well, then you're going to cut down your competition immensely and have a good chance of making it in the music business.

Here's a list of some books that may help you practice your reading:

Method For Clarinet, by H. Klose ($8.50 from Carl Fischer, 62 Cooper Square, New York, NY 10003). This book is only for single-note reading but since the clarinet and guitar have basically the same range it is an excellent study.

Develop Sight Reading, Vols. 1 and 2, by Gaston Dufresne ($3.50 each from Chas. Collin Music, 315 W. 53rd St. New York, NY 10019). This is also for single-note reading, but if you can get through the complete book you've got it made.

Rhythms Complete, Vols. 1, 2, 3, and 4, by Bugs Bower ($3.95 each from Chas. Colin).

Progressive Steps To Syncopation For The Modern Drummer, by Ted Reed $3.00 from Ted Reed, Box 327, Clearwater, FL 33515). This book is great for part 3 of the test that we just covered.

Basic Jazz Conception For Saxophone, Vols. 1 and 2, by Lennie Niehaus ($6.95 each from Try Publishing, 845 Vine, Hollywood, CA 90038).

Advanced Duets, Vols 1, 2, and 3, by Bob Nelson ($7.50 each from Chas. Colin).

John McLaughlin And The Mahavishnu Orchestra ($8.95 from Warner Bros. Publ., 9200 Sunset Blvd., Suite 530, Los Angeles, CA 90069):

The Howard Roberts Guitar Book, by Howard Roberts and Jimmy Stewart ($6.00 from Playback, Box 4278, North Hollywood, CA 91607).

Joe Pass Guitar Style ($5.95 from Warner Bros.).

Finger-Picking Styles For Guitar, by Happy Traum ($3.95 from Oak Publ., 33 W. 60th St., New York, NY 10023).

Six Black Blues Guitarists, by Woody Mann ($4.95 from Oak Publ.).

Electric Bass Lines, by Carol Kaye ($18.25 for five volumes from Warner Bros.). This book is great for bass clef reading.

The Art Of The Folk Blues Guitar, by Jerry Silverman ($3.95 from Oak Publ.).

Carcassi Method For The Guitar, By G. C. Santisteban ($4.95 from Oliver Ditson Co., dist. by Theodore Presser, Lancaster and Presser Pl., Bryn Mawr, PA 19010).

Andres Segovia—Studies For The Guitar By Fernando Sor ($2.50 from Edward B. Marks Corp. dist. by Belwin-Mills, Melville, NY 11746).

The Lee Ritenour Book, by Lee Ritenour ($5.95 from Flat Five Publ., dist. by Professional Music Products, 1114 N. Gilbert St., Anaheim, CA 92801).

Eric Clapton Deluxe ($7.95 from Warner Bros.).

Jean—Luc Ponty ($8.95 from Warner Bors.).

The Jazz Styles Of Maynard Ferguson ($5.95 from Warner Bros.).

The Hal Leonard Guitar Method, Books 1-3, by Will Schmid ($3.95 each from Hal Leonard).

The Modern Approach to Classical Guitar, Books 1-3, by Charles Duncan ($5.95 each from Hal Leonard).

Bluegrass Method by Will Schmid ($4.95 from Hal Leonard).

Lead Rock Method, Vols. 1 & 2 by Al Clausea ($4.95 from Hal Leonard).

Finger Picking Solos Method, Vols. 1 & 2, by Will Schmid ($4.95 from Hal Leonard).

Blues Method, Vols. 1 & 2, by Robbie Slement ($4.95 from Hal Leonard).

This list goes to show you that reading everything and anything available will help you. Go to it, and believe me it will pay big dividends.

Lee Ritenour

HOW TO READ MUSIC

For some strange reason, reading music is a deep dark mystery to the majority of the uninitiated. It is not unusual for an adult with a degree in physics to walk into a studio to sign up for guitar lessons only, "if I don't have to learn to read music." This same person might be a bit embarrassed to learn the teacher has probably taught a couple of hundred second and third graders to read simple melodies in two or three lessons.

Anyone who is willing to memorize a few basics and practice consistently can learn to read music. Once you have learned, you can get rusty with inactivity, but you'll never forget how to read notes.

The Staff. The staff consists of five lines and four spaces (Figure 1).

The lines have names that are easy to learn by memorizing the following sentence. E vey G ood B oy D oes F ine   (Figure 3.)

The spaces also have names which spell the word FACE (Figure 2).

Figure 1.

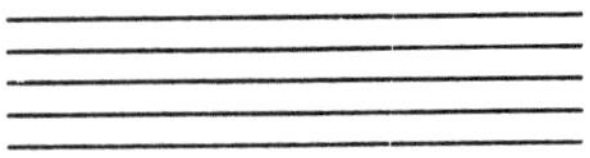

Figure 2.

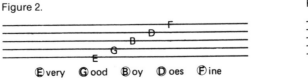

Ⓔvery   Ⓖood   Ⓑoy   Ⓓoes   Ⓕine

Figure 3.

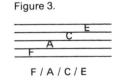

F / A / C / E

Ledger Notes. Sometimes notes are written above or below the staff with the use of ledger lines as shown below.

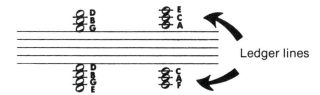

Ledger lines

The guitar student must become familiar with the notes *above* and *below* the staff as well as those *on* the staff. Speed in naming the notes in *any order* is important. The following exercise will help you learn the notes on the staff. Write in the name of each on the space below it.

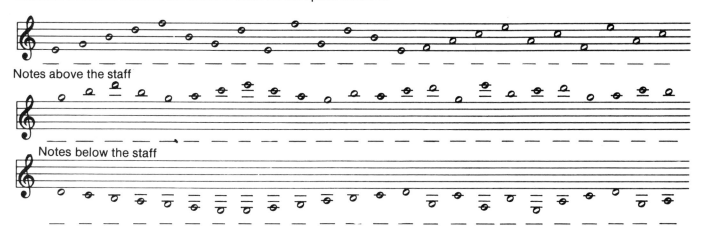

Notes above the staff

Notes below the staff

Pick up some music manuscript paper from your music store and make up your own exercises.

The G Clef. The notation explained thus far is all written in the G or treble clef, which is the clef used for guitar.

The G clef symbol circles the second line establishing *it* as G:

Notes. Notes are written different ways.  etc.

The different types of notes involving timing will be discussed later. Concentrate on the rapid naming of the notes on and below the staff. Your success in reading music depends on this!

The following shows where some of these notes are found on the guitar.
Caution: Do not confuse the five lines of the staff with the six strings on the guitar:

1st String

Fingering
0   1   3

OPEN   FRET 1   FRET 3

Play each note until you have a mental picture of it. Say the names aloud. Now try the exercise:

Memorize the notes on strings two and three as shown below.

2nd string

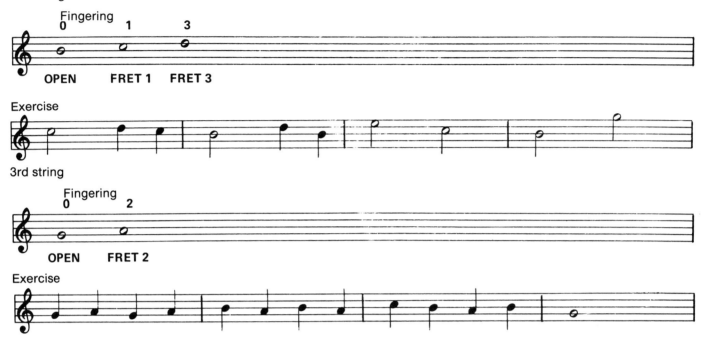

Exercise

3rd string

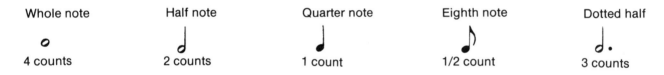

Exercise

So that the player knows how long to hold a note before proceeding to the next, each type of note is assigned a value. In the popular time signatures such as 4/4, 3/4, 2/4 and C (common time) the values are assigned as follows:

Whole note	Half note	Quarter note	Eighth note	Dotted half
𝅝	𝅗𝅥	𝅘𝅥	𝅘𝅥𝅮	𝅗𝅥.
4 counts	2 counts	1 count	1/2 count	3 counts

Memorize the above note values.

Many songs in the key of *C* and *G* can be played with the few notes covered so far. A book of songs for "easy guitar" will provide material for sight-reading practice.

GUITAR NOTATION vs. ACTUAL NOTATION

Actual pitch notation for the guitar refers to the use of both the treble and bass clef of the musical staff. Normally, guitar parts are transposed an octave higher than their actual pitch. This is done so that the guitarist can avoid mastering the bass clef altogether. I have never found any valid reason not to notate the guitar as it appears in the musical spectrum, especially since the guitar encompasses such a large percentage of the usable tonal range.

Most good studio musicians, so far as I know, use bass and treble clefs, or at least are capable of doing so. However, I believe that the average guitar player will reject the use of actual notation. It has been my sad experience that many guitar teachers are all too eager to reject something that they do not understand. In contrast, it has been my happy experience to find that music departments and guitar students at the college level are, in general, eager to accept and explore a new direction for the plectrum (pick style) guitar.

The use of actual pitch in writing for the guitar *is not my invention.* Any legitimate arranger or composer who did not know of the traditional one octave transposition used in writing for the instrument would unquestionably write for the guitar in *actual pitch*, especially given the true range of the instrument, which encompasses both treble and bass clefs. The twentieth-century composer Arnold Schoenberg wrote the guitar part in actual pitch in his *Serenade* Op. 24.

The most restrictive aspect of music written for the plectrum guitar in traditional *guitar notation* is that it places the instrument's range in the treble clef, like the rhythm banjo. Often, this results in the misnaming of chords by the composer or arranger whenever possible, in place of the guitar part. Some examples of misnamed chords are:

Calling a major sixth a minor seventh, and vice-versa.

Calling a ninth chord a minor sixth, and vice-versa.

Calling an augmented chord by any note of the chord.

Calling a diminished seventh chord by any note of the chord thereby (as in the augmented chord) completely destroying the understanding of the use of the chord, and the utilization of these chords as upper particles of the more intricate harmonizations (e.g. 7b5 [aug. 11]; altered ninth chords).

The major drawback to using *guitar notation,* aside from the ridiculous use of ledger lines in high positions, is that it leaves the guitarist, student, and teacher completely out in the woods about what to do, what to believe, and what to teach to achieve a good basic understanding of music. Guitar notation creates the appalling misconception for the guitarist that he does not have to concern himself with what the correct bass note being played by the bassist and pianist is. Guitar notation also gives the guitarist the impression that he can indiscriminately invert the bass note of any chord without the slightest awareness that he thereby commits one of the most fundamental musical no-nos—playing undesirable close intervals in the bass clef.

Using *actual pitch notation* fosters unity in thinking between the guitarist, bassist, and pianist. Composers and arrangers writing for the guitar in actual pitch seem to have a much better understanding of the instrument harmonically. By not understanding the guitar in its true musical spectrum there is no way, other than luck, that the guitarist can create harmonized melodies (chordal fill-ins) if he is not absolutely sure and cognizant of the *bass note.*

When we examine the comparatively short history of the plectrum guitar, we find that during any given period in its development, there have been only a few notable guitarists. In my opinion, these were people whose gift of music pulled them through in the absence of good teachers.

Even now, it is almost impossible for a serious student of the guitar to get the kind of quality musical experience necessary to turn out a truly professional player and teacher. Actual pitch opens up a new realm of music literature and helps break the bonds that tie the serious guitarist to the music written or transcribed only for the guitar.

Johnny Smith

'Born Free'   John Barry

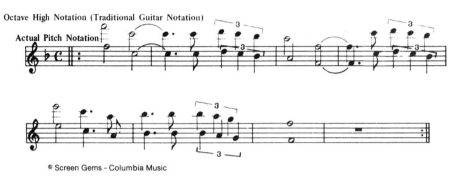

© Screen Gems - Columbia Music

TABLATURE: ALTERNATIVE GUITAR NOTATION

Simply put, tablature—or tab—is an easy-to-read system of music notation for fretted instruments utilizing a graphic representation of the strings with numbered fret positions, rather than a conventional staff with notes. In use in various forms since the 16th century, tablature has served to make published music for instruments such as the guitar, lute, banjo, and mandolin accessible to players who don't read standard music notation.

See Figure 1 for an example of tablature for the vihuela (a predecessor of the guitar) from a piece entitled "Guardame Las Vacas," written in 1538 by Luis de Narvaez.

Minor variations in early tablature include the use of letters instead of numbers, and the positioning of letters *between,* rather than *on,* the lines.

Currently, there is little tablature for jazz and certain other styles, and even less for classical. Generally, classical and jazz are more formally taught than, say, folk or rock, and thus the ability to read standard notation may facilitate a grasp of music theory required by some students. Many repertoire and method books on folk, blues, and rock guitar, however, include tablature of a combination of tab and standard notation, as do certain of the monthly instructional columns in *Guitar Player.*

Figure 1.

Lines And Numbers. Guitar tablature uses a system of six lines, each of which represents a string on the instrument. The bottom line corresponds to the 6th (*E*), or lowest-sounding string. The remaining five lines represent the other five strings. (*A, D, G, B,* and *E,* low to high). To avoid confusion, remember: *There is no direct relationship between the guitar's strings and the lines of a conventional music staff.*

Like chord diagrams and regular notation, tablature requires that the student spend a little time getting used to the relationship between what's on paper and what's on the guitar. Once you get your bearings, tab will likely prove convenient and useful. Figure 2 demonstrates the correlation between a chord diagram and its tab counterpart.

Figure 2.

A number is used in tablature to indicate at which *fret* the designated string is to be played. For instance, a "0" means to play the string *open;* a "1" indicates the 1st-fret position; a "2" designates the 2nd fret; and so on. It becomes apparent, then, that any succession of notes can be obtained by positioning a series of numbers on the appropriate lines. For example, here is a *C* major scale starting on the fifth string and ending on the second string (see example 1). Two or more notes to be played simultaneously are aligned vertically, as shown in this example of a *C* chord (see Example 2).

Rhythmic Notation. Rhythmic notation is include in tablature in either of two ways. It can be shown directly on the tab staff—as in Example 3, or by having the coinciding standard notation directly above the tablature as shown in Example 4.

A basic understanding of rhythms is helpful, especially when learning unfamiliar material. Many tab books either assume the player's familiarity with the song (especially in pop or folk music), or they include or make available a record or tape of the material to acquaint the student with the tune before trying to play it.

Hammer-Ons And Pull-Offs. The letters "H" and "P," for hammer-on and pull-off, respectively, indicate when these techniques are to be used. A tie, connecting the notes to be hammered-on or pulled-off, serves as a reminder that only the first note should be picked by the right hand (see Example 5). Here is a phrase using a combination of consecutive hammer-ons and pull-offs as shown in Example 6.

Slides. Slides are designated by the letter "S" and a straight line joining the note being slid *from* and the note being slid *to*. The angle of the line varies depending on whether the slide is ascending or descending. As with a hammer-on, only the first note is struck with the right hand (see Example 7). A wavy line is used to indicate a slide from an indeterminate point to a specific note (see Example 8).

Bends. Bends of a half-step are indicated with a curved line as in Example 9.

Bends of a whole-step are shown with a curved line followed by the tab number (in parentheses) denoting the pitch you're bending to (see Example 10).

A reverse bend—in which (1) the string is bent, (2) the note is struck, and (3) the string is allowed to return to the left of the fret number appears in Example 11.

Example 1.

Example 2.

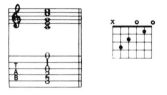

Example 3.

Example 4.

Example 5.

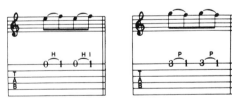

Example 6.

Open Tunings. In conventional notation, a piece written for a non-standard tuning can be both confusing and frustrating. Once a string is retuned, notes normally corresponding to certain frets will shift relative to the degree of retuning. But since tab is written with fret numbers rather than note symbols, all pieces are read in the same way, *regardless of the tuning* (see Examples 12 and 13).

Finally, keep in mind that certain aspects of tablature (as well as conventional notation) are not standardized, and a bit of imaginative interpretation is sometimes called for. Fortunately, though, most tablature is consistent enough so that minor variations can be easily accommodated.

Jim Ferguson

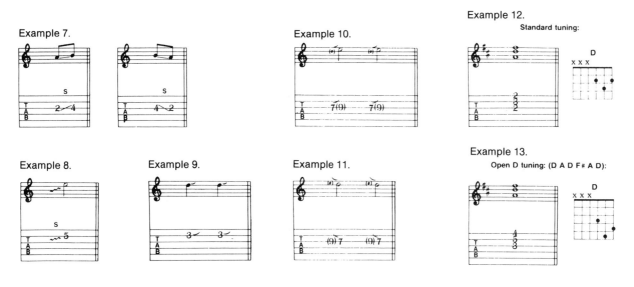

Example 7.

Example 8.

Example 9.

Example 10.

Example 11.

Example 12.
Standard tuning:

Example 13.
Open D tuning: (D A D F♯ A D):

'Greensleeves'

Trad., arr. by Jim Ferguson

4. TUNING

Example 1.

Example 2.

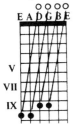

Example 3.

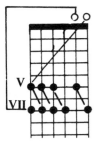

TUNING UP

Standard Method. To begin with, there is the standard method given in most guitar instruction books. First you find a reference note (low *E*) on the piano, with a tuning fork (A-440), or some other device. Once you have tuned one of your strings to the reference note, you may begin to tune the rest of the strings. If it was a low *E* reference note which you tuned your sixth (thickest) string to, you then depress the low *E* (sixth) string at the 5th fret and tune your *A* (fifth) string to match the tone sounded by your low *E* string depressed at the 5th fret. Next, depress the *A* string at the 5th fret and tune your *D* (fourth) string to the tone sounded on the *A* string (5th fret). Next, depress the *G* string at the *4th* fret and tune your *B* (second) string to the tone sounded by the *G* string at the 4th fret. Then, finally, depress your *B* string at the 5th fret and tune your high *E* (first) string to that tone. (See Example 1.)

***D* Note Method** (A Good Check). Another method of tuning is the *D Note Method* since the system utilizes the *D* (10th fret) on the low *E* (sixth) string. With this method, often times used as a check, you first tune your low *E* string to some reference instrument or device. Once the low *E* is tuned to proper pitch, you depress it at the 10th fret and compare the tone sounded to the tone sounded by playing the *D* (fourth) string open. The two should sound the same. Next, depress the *A* (fifth) string at *G* (10th fret) and compare the tone of that note with the *G* (third) string played open. Next, depress the *D* (fourth) string at *B* (9th fret) and compare that pitch to the tone produced by playing the *B* (second) string open. And finally, depress the *G* (third) string at *E* (9th fret) and match that tone with the high *E* (first) string. Because this method takes place in the upper register of your instrument, it is a good method for lead guitarists to check their tuning by. (See Example 2.)

Harmonic Method. Perhaps the most commonly used tuning method among career guitarists is the *Harmonic Method* which used the belltone sounds of the instrument in the tuning process. Harmonics may be produced by touching a string lightly with a left hand finger above certain frets of the guitar without depressing the string, and with a right hand finger (placed close to the bridge) picking the string. (The easiest harmonic to produce is played by placing a left hand finger directly over the 12th fret of any string, and picking that string close to the bridge.)

The harmonic method utilizes the harmonics played on the 5th and 7th frets. Once you have tuned your low *E* (sixth) string to a reference instrument or device, place your first finger (left hand) directly over the 5th fret of the low *E* (sixth) string and sound a harmonic with your right hand finger or plectrum. You then place your third finger (left hand) on the 7th fret of the *A* (fifth) string and produce a harmonic. These two harmonics should sound the same; if not, adjust the *A* string.

Next, sound a harmonic with your first finger (left hand) directly over the 5th fret of the *A* (fifth) string and compare it to the harmonic sounded when you place your third finger (left hand) directly over the 7th fret of the *D* (fourth) string. Then, sound a harmonic with your first finger placed directly over the 5th fret of the *D* (fourth) string and match it with the harmonic sounded by your third finger placed directly over the *G* (third) string at the 7th fret.

To tune the *B* string, sound a harmonic directly over the 7th fret of the low *E* (sixth) string and compare it to the *B* (second) string played open.

To tune the high *E* (first) string, you have two choices. You may either sound a harmonic with your first finger directly over the 5th fret of the *B* (second) string and compare it to a harmonic sounded by placing your third finger directly over the 7th fret of the high *E* (first) string; or, sound a harmonic with your first finger over the 5th fret of the low *E* (sixth) string and compare it to the fifth *E* (first) string played open. (See Example 3.)

It is important that you listen carefully to the tones produced by harmonics, for it usually takes the beginner a while to hear the tone well. Also, the harmonic method of tuning requires that your strings be relatively new, otherwise the method will simply de-tune your guitar.

Michael Brooks

HOW TO CORRECT TUNING DEFECTS

We have discussed several methods of tuning and if you have tried the systems, and your instrument still plays out of tune, you may have to correct some mechanical imperfections. Here are some common problems, how to locate them, and how they may be corrected.

Bad Strings. First check the strings. A simple test is to play the harmonic at the 12th fret of each string and compare it to the note produced at the 12th fret. In playing the tone be careful to put your finger straight down on the string and to not pull the string to either side. With the harmonics for reference, if *all* the natural notes are sharp or flat, your problem is with the intonation or action. If the discrepancies vary so some notes play sharp, while others play flat, and some are perfect, your problem is probably bad strings. In this case you may sometimes get a treble string to play in tune by rubbing it. This will get it hot and stretch it slightly in one area thereby balancing the string. If the natural note is sharp of the harmonic, rub the string from the 12th to the 1st fret; if it is flat, rub the string from the twelfth fret to the bridge saddle. If you still have strings that play out of tune, remove them and restring the instrument turning the strings around. Reverse one string at a time. Taking all the strings off at once causes a sudden change of tension for the soundboard which is not good for an instrument and may cause it to "go dead" for a while.

After the strings have had time to adjust, test them again. Throw away any that are still out of tune. The newness of a string has nothing to do with its trueness—often new ones are bad right out of the package. If you want your guitar in tune you will probably have to throw away an occasional string.

If the harmonics and natural notes at the 12th fret are in tune, and the guitar still plays out of tune, the problem is probably misplaced frets. You may test the fret position by playing several different scales on a single string, preferably a treble string. If any interval sounds out of tune you may further doubt the fret placement.

Bad Intonation. Even the finest guitars do not always have perfect intonation. If you simply cannot tune your instrument, and the discrepancy between the harmonics produced at the 12th fret and the corresponding natural notes is always in the same direction (i.e. the notes are always sharp or always flat), you may be fairly certain that either the saddle, nut, or the fret placement is incorrect. At this point you may wish to go straight to a good repairman to have your instrument adjusted. If you cannot go to a repairman, or if you would like to know how to fix the guitar yourself, here is how to locate and correct the problems of intonation:

1. Measure the distance from the nut to the 12th fret. (Always measure from where the string leaves the nut or saddle, and measure to and from the center line of frets.)
2. Measure the distance from the 12th fret to the saddle.
3. The distance from the 12th fret to the saddle should be used about 1/16" (1.5mm) longer than the treble side. On guitars with an especially high action on the bass side (as with a Ramirez), the bass may be .020" (.5mm) to .030" (.75mm) longer on the bass side than on the treble side. If the nut and the saddle seem to be properly situated, and your strings are true, and you still have tuning problems, the error is probably in the fret placement.
4. The saddle is misplaced if the distance from the 12th fret to the saddle is *not* longer than the distance from the nut to the twelfth fret. At least 75% of tuning problems involving bad intonation are caused by incorrectly set saddles. Minor adjustments can be made sometimes by simply changing the radius on the saddle bone. More serious adjustments might involve filling the saddle slot and recutting it, or actually moving the bridge. Before adjusting the saddle it is prudent to check the nut position, because if you correct a misplaced nut you may also cause the saddle to be in its proper position. If, however, you find the nut and the 1st fret are perfectly placed, you may assume your tuning problems are caused by the saddle bone, and you may adjust it.
5. An essential measurement for checking the fret and nut placement is the *basic string length*, which I shall refer to as B.S.L. This is the distance from the nut to the 12th fret multiplyed by two.
6. To compute the correct distance from the nut to the 1st fret divide B.S.L. by 17.81715, a constant I shall refer to as *C*.
7. Measure the actual distance from the nut to the 1st fret. If it is the same as the theoretically correct difference, or if it is shorter up to .045" (1.12mm), the 1st fret is properly placed.
8. If the actual length is shorter then the theoretical length, or if it is shorter than .045" (1.12mm), the nut is probably misplaced. You will do well to check the placement of a few more frets before adjusting the nut.
9. The placement of the remaining frets can be computed in the same way the distance from the nut to the 1st fret was determined; i.e., take the calculated distance from the nut to the previous fret, subtract it from the B.S.L. and divide by *C* to determine the correct distance from any fret to the one preceding it. Thus the correct distance from the 1st fret to the 2nd fret is computed by subtracting the calculated distance from the nut to the 1st fret from B.S.L. and dividing by *C*.
10. If the actual placement of frets differs from the correct placement by a fairly constant sum in the first few frets, say, .050" (1.25mm), you may suspect the nut is misplaced by that approximate sum.
11. To check your assumption subtract the sum, .050" (1.25mm) in the hypothetical case mentioned in step 10, from the distance from the nut to the 12th fret. Multiply this by 2 to compute a new B.S.L.
12. Recompute the correct fret placement using the new B.S.L.
13. Compute what the actual fret placement would be if the nut were moved to the place from which you compute the new B.S.L.
14. If the newly computed actual fret placement and the new correct fret placement are close, you may be sure the nut is improperly placed. Wood should be shaved off the end of the fingerboard, or added on, and the nut moved to its proper place. Nearly always when there is a problem of nut placement the nut has been set too far back.
15. You may now observe that by correcting the nut placement you have corrected an error in the placement of the saddle. You have changed the string length of the instrument. A .050" (1.25mm) correction in the nut will result on a .050" (1.25mm) correction of the saddle.

16. If the actual fret placement and the theoretical fret placement differ, but not by any constant, tuning problems are probably caused by misplaced frets. At the nut end of the fretboard a discrepancy of ±.025" (.62 mm) is still playable. The margin for error grows smaller as you go up the fretboard. At the 13th fret the margin is only ±.010" (.25 mm). There is a problem that must be corrected if two frets are misplaced by a permissible error, but in opposite directions. For instance an error of ±.020" (.5mm) at the 4th fret would be permissible as would an error of -.018 (.45mm) at the 3rd. The combination of errors is *not* okay however—in this situation chords that had notes on the 3rd and 4th frets would sound out of tune. The frets would need to be replaced.
17. Minor errors in fret placement can sometimes be corrected by moving the radius of the fret. Sometimes its slot needs to be filled, and a new one cut. If there are many problems it is best to replace the entire fretboard.

Fret Wear. Sometimes, though not frequently, tuning problems can be caused by frets that are flattened and worn. A good fret should have a centered, distinct radius. If frets are worn, they can cause small tuning problems, but, more important, they can cause problems in the action and tone of your guitar. A repairman can realign the radius on most frets and replace those he can't repair.

Tuning Problems Caused By Action Adjustments. If you have an extremely high action, or if your guitar was built with a high action that you lowered, you may have tuning difficulties. By moving the radius of the saddle slightly away from the soundhole on guitars where the action is raised, and moving the radius slightly towards the soundhole on guitars where the action has been lowered, you may correct these types of dilemmas.

A good repairman can assist you with tuning problems caused by bad intonation or action adjustments.

Michael Lorimer

5. CHORDS

CHORD CONSTRUCTION PRIMER

Example 1.

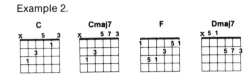

Example 2.

Whether it's in harmonizing a melody, finding an exotic embellishment, playing better solos, or just elaborating upon an existing grasp of chord usage, a good working knowledge of chord construction can only serve to make the guitarist a more complete musician. This article is not meant to be a comprehensive treatise on harmony, but rather a practical guide to chord construction for beginning and intermediate guitarists. While conventional notation is used for a number of the examples, the guitarist who doesn't read music can still learn the basics of chord construction.

Unfortunately, music theory is full of unavoidable ambiguities and inconsistencies—many of which can't be resolved in a way satisfactory to all theoreticians. However, this is understandable, considering that traditional harmony was never intended to accomodate many twentieth-century applications. After all, how could classical composers have foreseen a need to include chord symbols in their scores (as is common in current sheet music) so that one could supply an improvised accompaniment? Our system of terminology and analysis is somewhat inadequate for many everyday uses. However, with some basic information and reference tools, a guitarist can come to grips with these problems.

Upon mastering chord theory, many guitarists conclude that it's significantly less mysterious than they had anticipated, and sure enough, there's a good chance that you already know some of the required elements, even though you may need to view them in new ways in order to understand chord theory as such.

One basic element is the common "do, re, mi" scale with which you're likely already familiar. Each note in the scale is numbered. Our first example uses the *C* major scale, listed with its numbers and corresponding "do, re, mi" names. You'll notice that some notes are identified by two numbers (2/9; 4/11; 6/13), as in Example 1.

We'll explore the details of this scale and learn how to modify it by *raising* or *lowering* certain notes by half-step increments. Then we'll examine various groups (1, 3, 5; 1, 4, 5; and so on). Each group, or formula, yields a certain type of chord. Examples: a major chord consists of notes 1, 3, and 5, while a major 7th consists of 1, 3, 5, 7. Some familiar chords with scale-tone designations appear in Example 2.

Intervals. Much terminology used in music theory relates to the *diatonic* major scale, which is constructed from intervals of whole-steps and half-steps; a whole-step is a two-fret interval, while a half-step is a one-fret interval. In a *chordal* context, "diatonic" refers to notes occurring in a scale or mode, while "chromatic" pertains to notes that are not part of the prevailing scale of mode. (Regarding *scales*, "chromatic" commonly refers to *all* notes in succession—including diatonic notes; e.g.: C, C♯, D, D♯, E, etc.) Here is the whole-step/half-step pattern of the diatonic major scale (W =whole-step, 1/2=half-step):

W   W   1/2   W   W   W   1/2

The major scale's frequent use as a reference point is understandable, considering that it is historically the most commonly used and straightforward of scales. The names of intervals originate from the numerical order of notes in a scale. Therefore, the corresponding interval is called a *second*. E is the third note of the *C* scale; hence, it's distance from *C* is called a third. The naming sequence continues for all intervals.

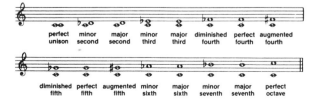

There are also names of intervals not naturally included in the major scale. They're easy to remember if thought of as *modifications* of the scale tones. Since one whole-step is equal to two half-steps, there must be a note between the two notes of a whole-step. For example, the whole-step of *C* to *D* has *D*♭ (also known as *C*#) in between. Complicating this, the intervals from *C* to *D* and *C* to *D*♭ are both called seconds.

You can see on your guitar that from *C* to *D* is a distance of two frets, while *C* to *D*♭ comprises only a one-fret distance. In order to differentiate between similar intervals, a *quality* of the intervals must be assigned. There are five basic types of intervallic qualities: major, minor, augmented, diminished, and perfect. The following chart shows the various intervals and the number of half-steps contained in them, as well as their qualities:

	Maj	Min	Perf	Aug	Dim
unison	--	--	0	--	--
second	2	1	--	--	--
third	4	3	--	--	--
fourth	--	--	5	6	4
fifth	--	--	7	8	6
sixth	9	8	--	--	--
seventh	11	10	--	--	--
octave	--	--	12	--	--

Note that after the seventh, the sequence repeats (i.e., unison=octave; second=ninth; third=tenth; etc.). Add 12 frets to any interval to produce a *compound* interval—an interval larger than one octave.

The following example includes the names of all the intervals relevant to chord construction; included are all intervals of the diatonic major scale up to the thirteenth:

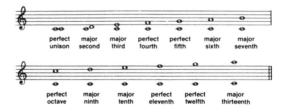

| perfect unison | major second | major third | perfect fourth | perfect fifth | major sixth | major seventh |

| perfect octave | major ninth | major tenth | perfect eleventh | perfect twelfth | major thirteenth |

Triads. By combining two or more intervals (three or more notes) and playing them simultaneously, one produces a chord. The most basic type, a *triad*, contains three different notes and consists of superimposed third intervals. Although constantly discussed in the context of the major scale, triads aren't necessarily derived from the major scale. Rather, unlike many other chords, they exist *naturally*, consisting only of scale tones and requiring no modification. But since terminology for all intervallic harmony does come from the major scale, we will refer to it in describing the construction of all chords.

There are four types of triads: major, minor, augmented, and diminished. They can be thought of as the basic building blocks of more complex chords. Triads, along with many other chords, are constructed by superimposing major and minor third intervals. The easiest way to remember and eventually catalog them is, once again, by thinking of them in terms of the major scale.

The major triad can be thought of as having this formula: 1, 3, 5. It consists of the first, third, and fifth notes of the major scale. The minor triad (called minor because it has a minor third in its makeup) is 1, ♭3, 5. The augmented triad, named for its augmented fifth interval between the root and fifth, is 1, 3, #5. (The #5 symbol in a chord is a substitute for the phrase "aug.") The diminished triad has a minor third and a diminished fifth interval, with a scheme of 1, ♭3, ♭5. It is commonly referred to as a flatted 3rd/flatted 5th. Example 3 shows examples that represent one way in which these simple triads can be played on the guitar.

For easy reference, the formulas for the four triads are:

> Major: 1   3   5
> Minor: 1   ♭3   5
> Augmented: 1   3   #5
> Diminished: 1   ♭3   ♭5

Some notes may be doubled, as is shown in Example 4.

Alterations And Extensions. As a preliminary to discussing the specifics of more complex chords, let's examine extensions and alterations. Extensions are so named because they are constructed of superimposed thirds beyond the basic triadic form. The numerical order of the tones created by superimposing thirds (i.e. 1, 3, 5, 7, 9, 11, 13) plays an important part in the naming of chords, but only if they are placed in the proper context (more on this later).

Alteration, the raising or lowering of a note by a half-step (one fret), is commonly used on the 5th and 9th. Chords that include such changes are referred to as *altered chords*. The most common way in which these alterations occur is: ♭5. #5, ♭9, #9. These can also be applied in various combinations: ♭5 ♭9, ♭5 #9, #5 ♭9, #5 #9.

Chord Families. Now that you have an understanding of the elements of fundamental chords, let's look at a logical way of subdividing the various chord types into manageable groups before proceeding to more complex variations. There are three basic families (or qualities) of chords: major, minor, and dominant. Major chords are characterized by the ♮3 (natural 3rd, or simply 3rd); minor chords by the ♭3; and dominant chords by the ♭7.

The Major Chord Family. The following points are generally true for major chords, as well as the other two chord families (all idiosyncrasies and exceptions will be noted):

1. When the fourth step of a major scale is added to a major or minor triad, the chord is called *suspended*, or *sus* (it is has no 3rd, it is neither major nor minor). A suspended chord generally consists of a 4th added to a chord, sometimes as a substitute for the 3rd. It creates a feeling of tension or non-resolution. Compare the sound of the *Csus* to the simple *C* chord (see Example 5).
2. Adding the sixth note of the scale to a chord creates a major 6th chord (commonly called 6th for short, as in *C6*, *F6*, etc.).
3. When the major chord is added to the triad, the chord is referred to as a major 7th.
4. If the major 7th is present in any chord, then the chord is referred to by its numerically highest member. For example, a chord with the formula, 1, 3, 5, 7, 9 would be called a major 9th. Now we enter into a rather vague area, because the chords named by the extensions 11th and 13th may *in theory* include all of the preceding tones (1, 3, 5, 7, 9, 11); however, *in practice*, it is common for some of these tones to be omitted.
5. The 4th is referred to as the 11th if the 7th is also present. For example, the formula for a *Cmaj11* is 1, 3, 5, 7, 9 (optional), 11. This type of extension is rarely used as a major chord.
6. The 6th is referred to as the 13th if the 7th is also present. For example, the formula for a *Cmaj13* is 1, 3, 5, 7, 9 (optional), 11 (rarely present), 13.
7. In adding the 9th (the same note as the 2nd) to a major triad, the

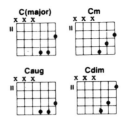

Example 3.

C(major)   Cm

Caug   Cdim

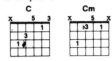

Example 4.

C   Cm

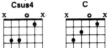

Example 5.

Csus4   C

extension is an add9 chord. For example, a *Cadd9*'s formula: 1, 3, 5, 9.
   8. A chord with both the 6th and the 9th, without the presence of the 7th, would be a 6add9 chord (1, 3, 5, 6, 9), as on *C6add9*.

Although extensions are generally voiced higher than other chord elements, it is not uncommon for them to occur in the lower register.

Special Situations.
   1. A relatively common alteration of a major chord (especially in jazz) is the #11. It may occur to you that the #11 is the same as the ♭5. However, it is more accurately called the #11 because the ♮5, 7, and 9 may be present in the chord as well.
   2. A chord having the formula 1, 3, ♭5 (an alteration not commonly found as a major chord) could be named ♭5 (e.g. *C♭5*) for lack of anything better to call it. Once you're familiar with all the basic terminology, you should find little difficulty in naming such uncommon chords.

The following list includes the symbols and formulas for all chords in the major family. Parentheses denote optional notes whose inclusion or omission will not affect the name of the larger chord. An asterisk (*) denotes chords that for theoretical purposes are considered only peripheral to the major family.

Major Chord Family Formulas	
Symbol	**Formula**
maj	1 3 5
sus*	1 3 (optional) 4 5
6	1 3 5 6
6add9	1 3 5 6 9
add9	1 3 5 9
maj7	1 3 5 7
maj9	1 3 5 7 9
maj11*	1 3 5 7 9 (op) 11
maj13	1 3 5 7 9 (op) 11 13
maj7#11	1 3 5 7 #11

The Minor Chord Family. The naming of minor chords is generally similar to the naming of major chords, except that minors have a lowered 3rd (♭3) instead of a natural 3rd. (♮3). Since the inclusion of the 7th is such a critical factor in naming certain extensions, let's first cover additions to the minor triad that do not include a 7th.

   1. Since the 4th can take the place of the 3rd, the suspended chord is more commonly thought of as major rather than minor, even though it can function in a minor capacity. It is often constructed in a 1, ♭3, 4, 5, format. For example, a *D* chord with both a 4 and ♭3 would be called *Dmsus*.
   2. Adding the 6th tone of the scale to a minor triad would change its name to minor 6th (as in *Cm6*).
   3. Although not common, a 2nd (9th) added to a minor triad (1, ♭3, 5, 9) creates a minor add 9 chord (e.g., *Cmadd9*). The 9th is often played in an upper register to de-emphasize the dissonance between the ♭3, and the 9.
   4. The inclusion of the 6th and 9th tones, but *not* the 7th, would yield a minor 6/9 chord (such as a *Cm6/9*).
   5. The 7th is most often lowered for minor chords, as well as in larger extensions. The abbreviation for this type would be *Cm7*, as in m7.

Subsequent extensions would include:

> m9: 1, ♭3, 5, ♭7, 9
> m11: 1, ♭3, 5, ♭7, 9 (op) 11
> m13: 1, ♭3, 5, ♭7, 9 (op) 11

Special Situations.

1. It is fairly common to lower the 5th of a minor 7th chord. This chord would be called *m7♭5* (minor 7 flat 5), also referred to as a *half-diminished* chord.
2. The addition of a major (not lowered) 7th to a minor triad would make the chord a minor/major 7th (as in a *Cm/maj 7*).
3. Although rare, especially beyond the 9th, extensions of minor/major 7th chords would be named similarly to extensions of minor 7th chords (numbers in parentheses represent optional notes):

> m/maj7: 1 ♭3 5 7
> m/maj9: 1 ♭3 5 7 9
> m/maj11: 1 ♭3 5 7 (9) 11
> m/maj13: 1 ♭3 5 7 (9) (11) 13

The following is a list of the members of the minor family, their symbols, names, and formulas:

Minor Chord Family Formulas	
Symbol	**Formula**
m	1 ♭3 5
msus	1 ♭3 4 5
m6	1 ♭3 5 6
m7	1 ♭3 5 ♭7
madd9	1 ♭3 5 9
m6/9	1 ♭3 5 6 9
m9	1 ♭3 5 ♭7 9
m11	1 ♭3 5 ♭7 9(op) 11
m13	1 ♭3 5 ♭7 9(op) 11(op) 13
m/maj7	1 ♭3 5 (♮)7
m7♭5	1 ♭3 ♭5 ♭7

The Dominant 7th Family. Basically, a dominant 7th chord, most commonly referred to simply as 7th, is a major triad with a lowered 7th added. The dominant 7th family has many more chords than either the major or minor families, due to the large number of extensions and alterations, plus potential combinations of both. The formula for the dominant 7th chord is: 1, 3, 5, ♭7. Extensions of the 7th chord include:

> 9th: 1 3 5 ♭7 9
> 11th: 1 3 5 ♭7 (9) 11
> 13th: 1 3 5 ♭7 (9) (11 rare) 13

Remember that for major and minor as well as 7th (♭7) chords, it is common to refer to a chord simply by the number of the highest extension, even though other extensions are present in the voicing. In many voicings, it is common to eliminate the optional tones.

There are more alterations for ♭7 chords than any other type. These can also be in numerous combinations with each other as well as with the various extensions. The following list includes only a few of the many possibilities. Common sense can be employed in naming other alterations not mentioned here.

7#5: 1 3 #5 7
7b5: 1 3 b5 b7
7#9: 1 3 5 b7 #9
7b9: 1 3 5 b7 b9
9#5: 1 3 #5 b7 9
9b5: 1 3 b5 b7 9
7#5 #9: 1 3 #5 b7 #9
7#5 b9: 1 3 #5 b7 b9
7b5 #9: 1 3 b5 b7 #9
7b5b9: 1 3 b5 b7 b9

Special Situations.
1. Although it can be argued that the augmented and diminished triads, plus the diminished 7th chords, could be put in their own separate categories (the diminished and augmented triads don't even have 7ths added to them), they have been included here because they most often *function* as dominants in chord progressions.
2. The diminished 7th has a double-flatted 7th (lowered one whole-step; the bb7 is equivalent in pitch to the major 6th).
3. It is common for the 3rd to be omitted from dominant 11th chords.
4. A b5 chord is more accurately called #11 if the natural 5th is included.

Here is a list of chords in the dominant family (an asterisk denotes a chord that for theoretical purposes is thought of only as a peripheral relative of the dominant family):

Dominant 7th Family Chord Formulas	
Symbol	**Formula**
7	1 3 5 b7
9	1 3 5 b7 9
11	1 3(op) 5 b7 9(op) 11
13	1 3 5 b7 9(op) 11(op) 13
7#5	1 3 #5 b7
7b5	1 3 b5 b7
7b9	1 3 5 b7b9
7#9	1 3 5 b7 #9
dim*	1 b3 b5
dim7*	1 b3 b5 bb7
aug*	1 3 #5
7#11	1 3 5 b7 9(op) #11

Practical Notation. There are some notational problems that are especially difficult to resolve. For instance, if the 9 and 11 are optional in a 13th chord, then how do you know when it is appropriate to include them? The answer is: You don't. In playing the changes to popular tunes from song books or chord charts, some guesswork is unavoidable.

However, in working out chords, much more specific ways of notating them can be employed if you use a little thought and learn to simplify things as much as possible. For instance, even though you know that in theory the 9th can be included in a 13th chord, try to be more specific when writing it out. It could be more clearly written as a 9add6 (the 6th is the same as the 13th). Even though calling it a 13th is technically correct, referring to it as a 9add6 is more specific. Also, when a specific bass note is required, it can be written as an attachment to a chord symbol; e.g. C/G, where C is the chord and G is the specified bass note (see Example 6).

Voicings And Omitted Tones. The terms "voicing" and "inversion" are often used interchangeably. However, the inversion refers to the lowest note sounding in the chord (whether it's the root or not). A chord with the root as the lowest note is said to be in root position; with the 3rd as the

Example 6.

C/G

Example 7.

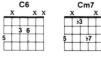

C6   Cm7

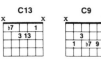

C13   C9

Example 8.

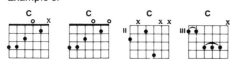

lowest note it's called first inversion; with the 5th as the lowest note it's called second inversion; and with the 7th as the lowest note it's called the third inversion.

Voicing, though, denotes the order of tones in a particular chord. Let it suffice to say that there are many possible voicings for any one chord. A 13th chord, for instance, can include as many as seven different tones. But, how is it possible to play a chord like that in a 6-string guitar? It isn't. In order to make many chords playable, certain tones must be omitted. The most important tones are the 3rd and, when dealing with the extended chords, the 7th. The 3rd differentiates a major chord from a minor one, and the 7th differentiates a major-type chord from a dominant 7th. Other notes that must be included are those critical to describing the chord's *quality*. For example, a 9th chord must have a 9th, a 3rd, and a ♭7th. A minor 11th would require a ♭3rd, a ♭7th and an 11th. Consequently, the least important notes are the 5th and the root, respectively. Although traditional keyboard theory maintains that the root must be present (even if supplied by another instrument), rootless chords are quite common on the guitar. Either the root or the 5th has been left out of the chords shown in Example 7.

Examples of chords of the same inversion with different voicings are illustrated in Example 8.

Alternate Symbols. Most attempts at standardizing the notation of chord symbols have been futile, and a wide variety is still being used, creating a potential for confusion when reading music from diverse sources. The following is a list of some commonly used symbols:

1. Major 7: maj7, ⊽, △7, M7, Maj7 (Extensions of major seventh chords would be notated in a similar fashion; i.e., for major 9th: maj9, ⊽, △9, M9, Maj9, etc.)
2. Minor: min, -, m
3. Minor 7: m7, mi7, -7
4. Minor 7♭5: m7♭5, o
5. Augmented: aug, +
6. Diminished: dim, o

Final Notes. To gain a clearer understanding of the preceding material, find exercises and everyday situations in which to apply your newly acquired knowledge. For instance, practice constructing different voicings of the same chord. Example 9 shows some different voicings of a *Cmaj7* chord (you needn't restrict yourself to the first position).

Example 10 gives you some additional chords with their scale tone designations. Remember: The *G* family of chords is based on the *G* scale, the *D* family on the *D* scale, etc.

Also, determine the relationships between a tune's melody and its basic chords, such as in this example of the first few bars of "House Of The Rising Sun":

Combining a basic knowledge of chord formulas with hands-on experience will reveal that there is in fact a purpose behind many of these seemingly abstract concepts. Check your local library's music section, or browse through the material at the music store. You're bound to find plenty of literature to guide and strengthen your approach to chords.

Jim Ferguson and Tom Mulhern

Example 9.

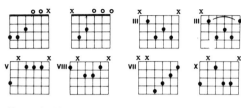

Example 10.

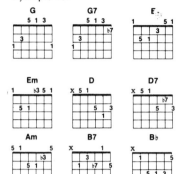

ALTERNATE CHORD FINGERINGS FOR BEGINNERS

The *D* Chords. One of the sources of confusion for many beginning guitarists is the fact that a number of basic chords may—and often should—be fingered in a variety of ways, each of which serves a different function. These aren't different chord patterns or inversions of the same chord, but the *same* chord pattern. Chord playing is not static; rather, it is a dynamic process. A chord functions in an ever-changing milieu, and chords progress from one to another. Learning alternate fingerings of basic chords becomes important in facilitating progressions, to get those fingers moving smoothly from one chord to another.

One of the first chords that most guitarists learn is *D* major, and it is almost invariably fingered as shown in Example 1.

There will be a time, however, when the D major chord will need to be changed to *D7*—perhaps on the way to *G* major or, in a blues, to be changed back and forth between *D7* and *D*. While certainly possible, the first fingering you learned is obviously not best suited for this progression. Try the one shown in Example 2.

Example 1.

Example 2.   Example 3.

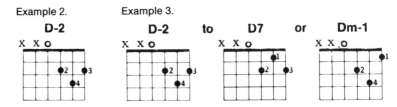

This alternate fingering shown in Example 3, not only makes the transition to *D7* much easier, but also smooths the way to an eventual *Dm*.

Another alternate *D* major fingering introduces a small barre over the first three strings, which facilitates the playing of the *A* note on the 5th fret of the first string (or *G♯* on the 4th fret) with the little finger of the left hand. This is indispensable for playing melodic passages on the first string while sustaining the chord (see Example 4).

Example 4.

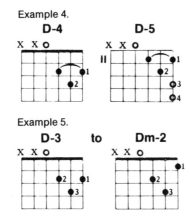

Example 5.

If the *D* chord moves rapidly to *Dm* and then back to *D* (but not to *D7*), as may happen in a blues-related song, there is still yet another possibility (see Example 5).

Note that the two fingerings for *Dm* are derived from the first two *D* major fingerings above. Let's see what possible advantages are afforded by each. In the first pattern, the *Dm* permits the unused 3rd finger to move freely to the notes *C* (fifth string, 3rd fret) and *F* (fourth string, 3rd fret). These two notes are melodically important in the key of *D* minor. In addition, *Dm-C-Dm* is a basic chord progression in many songs in *D* natural minor (*D, E, F, G, A, B*♭, C, D), *D* dorian (*D, E, F, G, A, B, C, D*), and the two forms of *D* pentatonic (*D, F, G, A, C,, D,* and *D, E, G, A, C, D*). (See Example 6.)

The other *Dm* fingering permits the unused 4th finger to play the *G* note (first string, 3rd fret). This added or suspended 4th (*G* is the fourth note of the *D* minor and major scales) is a characteristic sound in many arrangements (see Example 7).

If *D* was the first chord you learned, then *A7* was probably the second. There are two basic *A7* patterns, each of which has fingering variations. The simplest is played as shown in Example 8.

This fingering moves directly to the first *D* chord we looked at. But what if we wanted to move to the second or third fingering we examined? (See Example 9.)

Example 6.

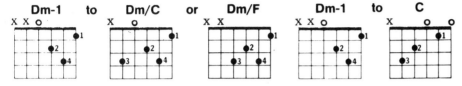

Example 7.

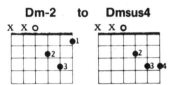

Example 8.

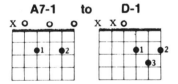

Example 9.

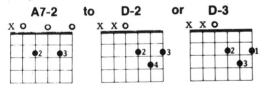

Example 10.

Example 11.

The G Chord. The next chord we will consider is G (see Example 10). Fingered as shown, this chord generally causes some difficulty for the beginner or small child, due to the relatively long stretch between the 2nd and 3rd fingers. As a result of this difficulty, very often the note G on the 3rd fret of the first string is completely muffled (resulting in an unpleasant alternative). If the 4th finger is substituted for the 3rd, however, a number of benefits are immediately realized (see Example 11).

Most obviously, the long stretch between the sixth and first strings can be fingered more easily despite the fact that in the early stages of guitar playing, the 4th finger is the weakest member of the team.

For the more advanced guitarist, however, freeing the 3rd finger can offer interesting possibilities. The 3rd finger can roam over the fourth, third, and second strings, producing on the 3rd fret of each of these strings, respectively, F, Bb, and D. Added to a G chord, the F note creates a G7. Bb is useful in many picking situations, especially where it contrasts with the open B string. D is a useful melodic note within a G chord, and it also produces the "open" or G5 chord form (see Example 12).

Example 12.

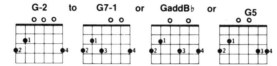

The following alternate fingering for G is recommended when the chord moves to G7 and then on to C. Although beginners have great difficulty with this pattern because of the stretch between the 2nd and 3rd fingers, the benefits are well worth the effort and initial discomfort (see Example 13).

Example 13.

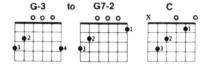

The A-Chord. The A major chord offers a number of distinct fingering possibilities. The form favored by many beginners involves the first three fingers. This pattern moves nicely to D (see Example 14).

Example 14.

People with large fingers sometimes have difficulties squeezing three fingers onto the same fret of neighboring strings. For that reason, as well as for the benefits realized by playing the chord with two fingers, this small barre version of the A chord is a useful pattern (see Example 15).

Example 15.

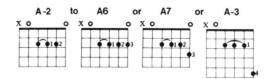

The alternate fingering for A major leads off comfortably in a number of diverse directions (see Example 16).

Example 16.

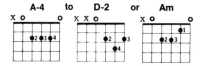

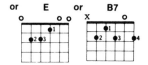

One more possibility comes to mind (see Example 17).

Example 17.

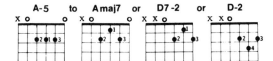

The E-Chord. E major offers similar possibilities. The "textbook" E favors changing to B7 and A (see Example 18).

Example 18.

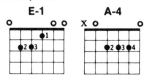

This variant leads more gracefully to barre chords (see Example 19).

Example 19.

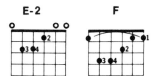

People with chubby fingers might like to try E this way (see Example 20).

Example 20.

This common C major chord fingering works well enough for most chord changes (see Example 21).

Example 21.

However, in the case of a rapid switch to certain barre chords, there is this possibility (see Example 22).

Example 22.

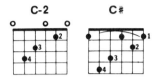

The alternate chord fingerings given here have just been suggestions. Obviously, your degree of skill will dictate the ease with which you go from chord to chord. Even if you are advanced, it is a good idea to reconsider basic concepts to see if there might be easier ways of fingering progressions.

Jerry Silverman

INVERSIONS: REACHING BEYOND THE 1ST FRET

Major and minor triads are composed of three notes each. These notes are arranged in a numerical relationship that can be expressed as 1, 3, 5 or, more properly, root, 3rd, and 5th. In simplest terms, this means that these chords are composed of the first, third, and fifth notes of their respective scales.

The difference between major and minor chords lies in the number of half-steps that separate the notes from each other. A major triad, for example, has its root separated from its 3rd by an interval of a *major third* (four half-steps); an interval of a *minor third* (three half-steps) lies between the 3rd and 5th. A *Cmaj* chord, or simply *C*, then, is composed of the notes *C, E,* and *G*. A minor triad has its intervals arranged in the opposite way. A minor third separates the root and 3rd, while a major third separates the 3rd and 5th. For a *Cm* chord, the notes are *C, E♭,* and *G*.

The order in which the notes of a chord are played, starting from the lowest (root, 3rd, 5th; or 3rd, 5th, root, or 5th, root, 3rd) is called the *inversion* of the chord. While basic chords are often presented with the root as the lowest note, *any* inversion may technically fulfill the chord function, although each inversion has its own distinctive flavor.

Inversions are not only easily played on the guitar, but they are extremely useful when played in movable patterns—especially on the upper three strings. These work well when combining melodies on the first string with chords. Now, let's examine the differences between the inversions.

Root position. In root position, the root is played as the lowest note. This is followed by the 3rd and 5th in ascending order. Here are the chords *C, D, Em,* and *Gm* in root position (see Example 1).

First inversion. The 3rd is the lowest note in a first-inversion triad. Above that are the 5th and root, respectively. Here are the four chords we just examined in first inversion (see Example 2).

Example 1.

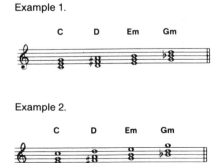

Example 2.

Second inversion. In this case, the 5th is the lowest note, followed by the root and the 3rd. Once again, we'll look at the same four chords, in yet another inversion (see Example 3).

Before we apply inversions to the guitar, it helps to know all the notes that are contained in the various major and minor triads. The following charts tell you what components make up these chords.

Example 3.

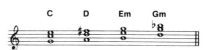

Notes of Major Chords			
Chord	**Root**	**3rd**	**5th**
C	C	E	G
G	G	B	D
D	D	F#	A
A	A	C#	E
E	E	G#	B
B	B	D#	F#
F#(Gb)	F#(Gb)	A#(Bb)	C#(Db)
C#(Db)	C#(Db)	E#(F)	G#(Ab)
Ab	Ab	C	Eb
Eb	Eb	G	Bb
Bb	Bb	D	F
F	F	A	C

Notes of Minor Chords			
Chord	**Root**	**3rd**	**5th**
Am	A	C	E
Em	E	G	B
Bm	B	D	F#
F#m	F#	A	C#
C#m	C#	E	G#
G#m(Abm)	G#(Ab)	B(Cb)	D#(Eb)
Ebm	Eb	Gb	Bb
Bbm	Bb	Db	F
Fm	F	Ab	C
Cm	C	Eb	G
Gm	G	Bb	D
Dm	D	F	A

Now we can pick up the guitar and see how the three inversions are played on the first three strings (E, B, and G). The root-position fingering (that is, the one with the root on the G string, the 3rd on the B string, and the 5th on the E string) looks as shown in Example 4.

Regardless of the fret location, the same root, 3rd, and 5th relationship will be maintained.

To determine the name of the chord being played in this formation at any given moment, you need but know the name of the three notes being played. If you are most familiar with the notes on the E string, then those notes will give you the 5th of the chord. Once you have established the 5th, you can easily locate the root. For example, if you play at the 3rd fret with either the major or minor pattern, the note on the E string will be a G. Therefore, the chord will be C (whether it is major or minor depends on the fingering you chose), since G is the 5th of C.

Now let's look at a first-inversion fingering pattern. This gives us the 3rd, 5th, and root on the G, B, and E strings, respectively (see Example 5).

If you utilize this form at the 3rd fret—with your 1st finger playing the note G on the E string—the chord will either be Gmaj (G) or Gm, depending on the pattern chosen; G is the root of both chords.

The second inversion is shown in Example 6. This form places the 5th, root, and 3rd on the G, B, and E, strings, respectively.

Example 4.

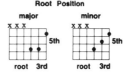

Example 5.

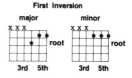

Example 6.

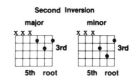

Example 7.

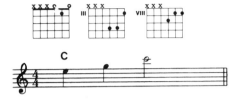

C

Example 8.

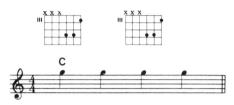

C

Example 9.

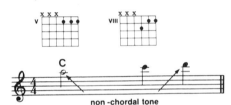

C

non-chordal tone

To determine the name of the chord created at any fret using this form, find what note is played on the first string. This will give you the 3rd of the chord, from which you can deduce the root by working backwards. For example, if you employ this major pattern at the 3rd fret, with your second finger playing the G note, the chord is an E♭maj (E♭). If the minor pattern is used, and your 1st finger is playing the G note on the E string, then the chord is Em.

With practice, you can apply these inversions to melodies. Incidentally, you may have been surprised to note that these three inversion patterns are not unfamiliar to you. In other words, you have been using inversions since you first learned to play chords.

Inversions ultimately give us the ability to select which note will be in the bass, middle, or upper voice of any given chord. For example, suppose you encountered a melody with the basic chord given as C. You might arrange this passage in chord-melody style (playing the melody with chords) as shown in Example 7.

Here are a few steps to help you further combine melody and chords.

1. It may be necessary to rewrite or at least visualize the melody an octave higher, or even go so far as to transpose the piece to a new key, so that most of all of the notes fall on the first string.
2. Determine if each note of the melody is part of the basic chord. Find the inversion that has the proper note in its upper voice.
3. Sometimes it may not be convenient to play a chord on each note of the melody. If not, try using chords on the first and third beats only, doing the rest of the melody as single notes (see Example 8).
4. Non-chordal tones may be played as either single notes or as substitutions for the uppermost voice of a chord (see Example 9).

The following song demonstrates the use of a simple chord melody. Pay close attention to the relationships between the chords and the melody line.

Jerry Silverman

'Johnny Has Gone For A Soldier'

Trad. arr. by Jerry Silverman

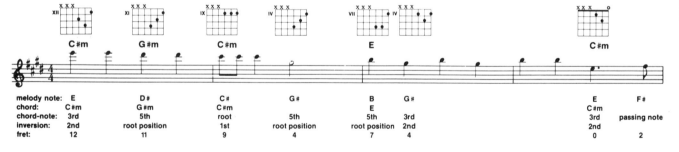

melody note:	E	D#	C#	G#	B	G#			E	F#
chord:	C#m	G#m	C#m		E				C#m	
chord-note:	3rd	5th	root	5th	5th	3rd			3rd	passing note
inversion:	2nd	root position	1st	root position	root position	2nd			2nd	
fret:	12	11	9	4	7	4			0	2

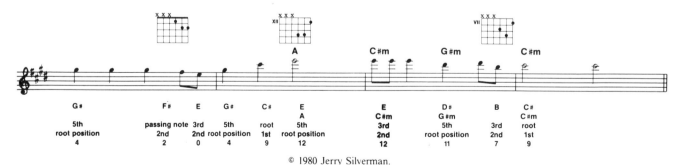

	G#	F#	E	G#	C#	E	E	D#	B	C#
						A	C#m	G#m		C#m
	5th	passing note	3rd	5th	root	5th	3rd	5th	3rd	root
	root position	2nd	2nd	root position	1st	root position	2nd	root position	2nd	1st
	4	2	0	4	9	12	12	11	7	9

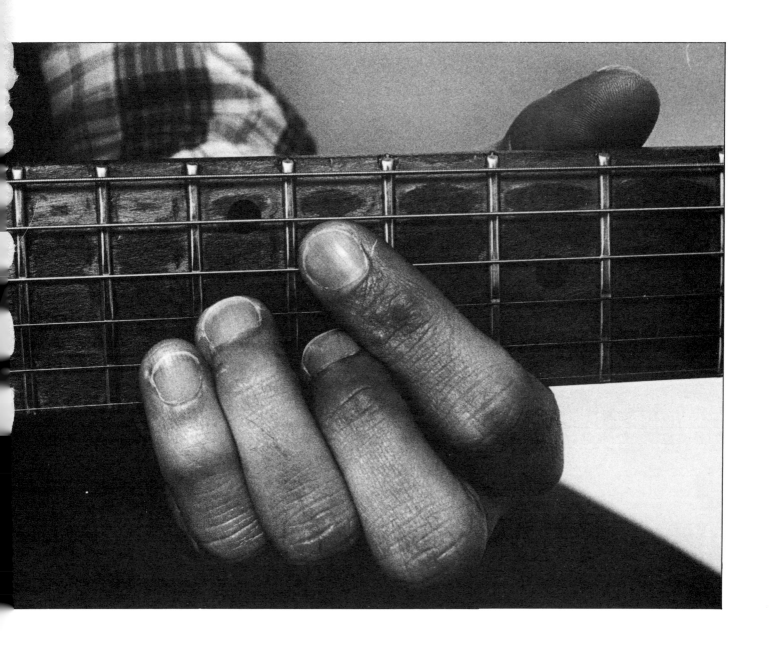

6. THE LEFT HAND

Example 1.

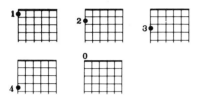

Figure 1.

Example 2.

Example 3.

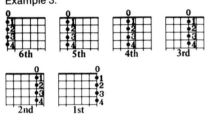

DEVELOPING THE LEFT HAND

Many of us are one-armed guitarists. We've mastered complex right-hand picking patterns, blues riffs, flat-picking runs and Calypso strums, but our chording fingers move like plump little Italian sausages. What do we do? After all, the best guitar player's chording hands seem to glide over the strings. Beautifully curved fingers seem to "type" out the proper notes on the frets. The little finger moves as gracefully as the other three digits. When a note demands the little finger, it attacks instantly. There is no thought of "using an easier finger." But how do we get this smooth? How do we learn to rocket around the neck machine-gun style?

Baxter to the rescue. I have discovered a handy-dandy exercise that will familiarize you with the fingerboard and make you both quick and confident. Here's how it works:

Divide the neck of the guitar into three basic areas, each having four frets. Now, with one being the index finger, two being the middle, three the ring, and four the little finger, and of course zero being "open" (unfretted), fret the following notes on the 6th string, one fret at a time. In other words, don't leave a finger on a string after you're through fretting it (see Example 1).

Here's the trick: Fret the string one note at a time and discover a placement of your thumb behind the neck where it remains in one place. The thumb shouldn't move every time you fret a different note on the 6th string. That slows you down. So decide on a place for your thumb which is similar to the illustration and stay there throughout the whole pattern (see Figure 1).

Dandy. Be sure the thumb is straight up and the pressure on the back of the neck is just above the middle joint of the thumb, on the fleshy pad. Put pressure on the thumb joint itself and you'll get a sore spot for sure.

Got a spot where your thumb stays put? Ok, now finger these notes one at a time, on the first string (see Example 2).

Don't move your thumb. It should stay in one place. In fact, it should stay in the same place whether you're fretting on the 6th string or the 1st string. That way the 1st four frets on each string are covered without slowing down to find a different left-hand position for each string. Find a single place for your thumb behind the neck and fret these notes on each string (see Example 3).

This is position number one. Try taking your hand clean away from the guitar neck and landing on the position one thumb spot. You'll get closer each time you try it.

Now let's try position number two which covers frets 5, 6, 7 and 8. Same idea as before; place your thumb somewhere between frets 6 and 7 and in the middle of the neck so you can easily get to each string and each fret without shifting the thumb position. One spot, no matter what string or fret you want in position two. Try the notes shown in Example 4.

Now you should have two basic positions for your thumb, which includes all the strings and every note from "open" to 8th fret. Ready? Let's try a quick drill and see if you can move in one flowing motion to either position one or position two and jam the correct finger on the indicated fret. For example, 6^1= fret the 6th string at the 1st fret with your index finger (position one). 6^8= fret the 6th string at the 8th fret with your little finger (second position). Go for the note in one shot. Don't break the movement into 1) finding the thumb position, 2) locating the correct finger, 3) fretting, and 4) moving the fretting finger next to the wire for a clear tone. *Do it all at once.* You can pick the note and sound it out if you want, but it would be better practice if you just work on the left, chording hand and go as quickly as you can without making noise. Here we go. Zoom, zip, zap and stab!

6^2, 6^3, 6^0, 6^4, 6^1, 6^0, (easy so far?) 5^1, 5^2, 5^3, 5^4, 5^5 (second position) 5^7 (ring finger in position two, remember?)5^8, 4^8, 3^8, 2^7, 2^6, 1^1 (yikes, big jump to position one!) 1^2, 1^3, 1^4, 1^3, 2^3, 2^4, 2^8, 2^7, 2^6, 2^1, 2^2, 3^0, 4^4, 4^5, 4^4, 4^5, 3^2, 5^5, 5^6, 5^7, 5^8, 4^0, 4^1, 3^2, 2^3, 2^1, 5^2, 5^6, 5^7, 5^8, (now you're getting it!) 5^1, 5^2, 5^3, 5^4, 4^0, 4^1, 4^2, 4^3, 4^4, 5^5, 6^2, 5^7, 5^8, 4^7, 4^8, 3^7, 3^6 . . .

Whew! You can really get moving from first position to second position, and your fingers really fly. By the way, what frets does your index finger fret? Right. 1 and 5. How about your little finger? Correct. 4 and 8. Ring? 3 and 7. Middle finger? Good. 2 and 6. Try this almost "yoga" exercise with no guitar. Concentrate on which finger frets which fret. Now, when I name a fret number see if you can actually feel the correct finger tense up, ready to go into action. You should actually feel energy entering the proper finger. Have a friend call out the numbers and close your eyes if you want. Here are the fret numbers; see what you can feel:

1, 3, 1, 3, 1, 4, 5, 6, 5, 6, 5, 6, 7, 8, 7, 8, 7, 2, 3, 2, 4, 2, 4, 5, 3, 5, 4, 5, 4, 1, 2, 3, 4, 5, 6, 7, 8, 7, 6, 5, 6, 7, 8, 7, 6, 5, 4, 3, 2, 1, 2, 3, 4, 5, 4, 3, 2, 4, 2, 7, 8, 7, 8, 5.

Did it work for you? Hope so. And I hope this whole exercise gives you some new speed and accuracy on the fingerboard. If you really want to push yourself you can add position number three; you'll have three places to put your thumb, and agility in fretting an entire octave on each string (see Example 5).

Keep in mind that the fingerings in positions one, two, and three aren't absolute. You can do finger runs, breaks and solos with your index starting at any fret (not just 1st fret, 5th and 9th like I've outlined), but for simplicity and quick movement to any string or fret follow my rules. For example, it's silly to finger a blues solo located only at the 7th and 8th frets with your ring and little finger. Use your index and middle, they're stronger. But as a general rule . . . oh, I'm sure you've got it straight.

Bob Baxter

Example 4.

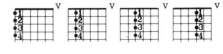

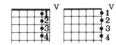

Example 5.

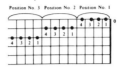

BASS RUNS

A bass run is a series of notes (played on the lower strings) that enhances the changes from one chord to another. Generally, the notes that make up the run are derived from the scale that connects the roots of the two chords involved. (The root of a chord is the note that gives the chord its letter name.)

In 2/4 and 4/4 time, the run usually begins two beats before the new chord is to be played. The run takes the place of the last two beats of the preceding chord and produces a smooth transition during the change. In 3/4 time, the run begins three beats before the arrival of the new chord, in the measure before the change.

The playing of bass runs greatly enhances the sound of an accompaniment and can lead eventually to the playing of melodies and counter-melodies.

For those of you who can't read music fluently, I will give the string and fret numbers, as follows: The first number is the string, and the second number is the fret. For example, 4/0 written beneath a note means that you should play the fourth string open; 5/2 is fifth string, 2nd fret, etc.

Here are some bass runs in 4/4 and 3/4 meters, shown in the commonly played keys of *C, G, D, A,* and *E* major (see Example 1).

Example 1.

Example 2.

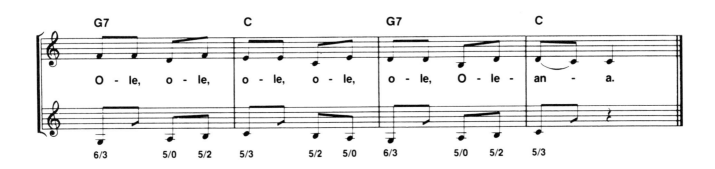

Bass runs add variety and interest to a vocal accompaniment. They interrupt the endless series of chords, which, no matter how skillfully played, might tend to become monotonous. However, in order to contribute to the overall musical effect, and not to inadvertantly detract from it, bass runs must be played tastefully and intelligently.

Bass runs are often the first individual notes (as opposed to chords) that a student will be asked to play. In the natural desire to play the run as quickly as possible, the tonal clarity of each note is often sacrificed in the interest of speed. Don't fall into this trap! Finger each note firmly and solidly with your left hand, while giving it a good lick with your pick or right thumb.

When you play runs in ascending scale order (e.g., *C* to *F*, *G* to *C*, *A* to *D*, etc.), keep the finger firmly pressing down on each note as you reach for the next higher note. If you let go of the lower note too soon, the run will have a choppy, staccato sound (and you will also hear the open string as you let go).

You must coordinate the movements of the hands so that the instant you finger the next note with the left hand, you strike the string with the right. If your timing is off in this respect, you will hear the next note twice—once when you finger it, and again when you pluck it.

Finally, it is not necessary to play a run every time one chord changes to another. Runs add variety only when they are employed *sparingly*, and not mechanically. A little seasoning can go a long way, but too much ruins the roast.

Example 2 shows the way a bass run may be added to the accompaniment of a song. (Note: 5/3 means fifth string, 3rd fret, etc.)

Jerry Silverman

HAMMERING ON AND PULLING OFF

Hammering On. A note may be played without picking by sharply striking a string with a left-hand finger. This technique is often referred to as *hammering on*. It is particularly useful and characteristic in certain types of accompaniments. Let's see how we approach the hammer-on. First, finger a *C* chord (see Example 1).

Keeping the 1st (index) and 3rd (ring) fingers down on their respective strings, lift the 2nd finger off of the fourth (*D*) string. Play this open string, then bring the 2nd finger down sharply to its original place at the 2nd fret, without picking the string with the right hand. You should hear the *E* note quite clearly. Next, follow the hammer-on with an up-pluck of the right-hand fingers as shown in Example 2 (play this on the first three strings).

We can make a complete strum out of this by preceding the hammer-on with a bass-chord strum. In this instance, the hammer-on is equivalent in time to two eighth-notes (of, say, an arpeggio). (See Example 3.)

Example 1.

Example 2.

Example 3.

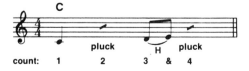

Try the same thing with a *G7* chord. The 2nd finger hammers-on at the 2nd fret of the *A* string (see Example 4).

Example 4.

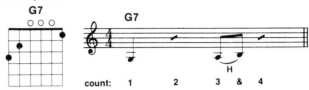

With an *F* chord, the 2nd finger hammers on at the third (*G*) string. The up-pluck is then executed with the 2nd and 3rd fingers on the second and first strings (*B* and *E*, respectively) as in Example 5.

Example 5.

In the exercise shown in Example 6, use the hammer-on as you have in the previous examples.

Example 6.

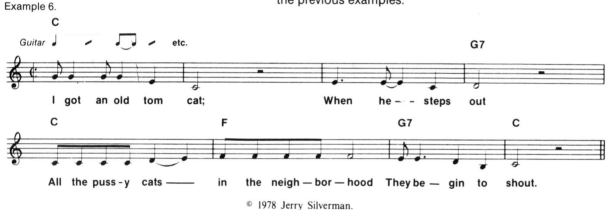

I got an old tom cat; When he – – steps out
All the puss-y cats ——— in the neigh—bor—hood They be—gin to shout.

Now let's try something a little different: a finger-strengthening exercise. We'll play an *E* major scale by hammering on from note to note. The right thumb will be used only to play the first note on each string (see Example 7).

Play this scale slowly and deliberately at first, bringing the full force of your fingers down on the strings. As you become more comfortable with this movement you'll be able to lighten those sledgehammer blows and speed up the passage from note to note. You can eliminate all the open strings (except the low *E*) by playing certain notes on the 5th fret of the appropriate strings. Follow the left-hand fingering carefully (Example 8).

Example 7.   Example 8.

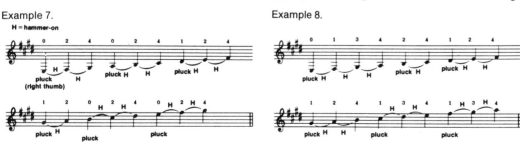

You can hammer-on a note even if the right thumb has not started the string vibrating. For example: With the 2nd (middle) finger on your left hand, hammer-on the *B* note on the *A* string (2nd fret) (see Example 9).

Now try this sequence of notes using only the left hand as shown in Example 10.

The five notes in the sequence were the plucked notes in the *E* major scale. You should now be able to play the entire scale (except for the first *E*) using only your left hand.

A *G* major scale can also be played in its entirety by hammering-on. You don't need the right hand at all, nor do you need open strings (see Example 11).

Pulling-Off. Since what goes up must usually come down, descending scales can be played in an analogous manner—by *pulling-off*. Let's work first with the natural notes—no sharps or flats. Finger the *G* note with the 3rd (ring) finger of the left hand on the high *E* string (3rd fret). Don't play anything yet, but prepare your 1st (index) finger on the *F* note (1st fret). Now play the *G*, and then actually pull the 3rd finger off the string. This pulling or plucking motion will cause the *F* note to sound. Now pull the first finger off *F* and the open *E* string will sound. Continue down, note-by-note and string-by-string (see Example 12).

Example 9.

Example 10.

Example 11.

Example 12.

Each of those plucked notes can be hammered-on so that, here again, the entire scale can be played just with the left hand.

For descending note passages played in this manner, open strings are to be sought after rather than avoided. They give the left hand a momentary rest and facilitate the movement from string to string. Consider the following (see Example 13).

When this descending pull-off sequence is combined with an ascending hammer-on, we have a little bit of blues (see Example 14).

Jerry Silverman

Example 13.

Example 14.

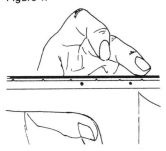

Figure 1.

Note that the right-hand finger is nearer than usual to the bridge.

There is no bend to the string as you lightly touch it. Note that the right-hand finger is nearer than usual to the bridge.

HARMONICS

One of the most natural, sweet-sounding "special effects" on the guitar is what we call a "harmonic." While many of you probably already know how to produce a harmonic on the guitar, the following lesson might serve to improve your technique for achieving the effect.

Natural Harmonics. Harmonics are delicate, sustained tones produced by lightly touching your left-hand finger to specific places on the string while it is being picked by your right-hand thumb, finger or plectrum. The theory goes something like this: Strings not only vibrate as a whole when you strike them, but they also vibrate in parts, such as halves, thirds, fourths and so on, producing what are called "overtones." At these junctures of vibration, where the overtones occur is where harmonics can be sounded (see Figure 2).

Figure 2.

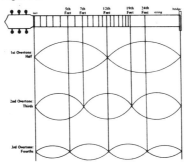

The first overtone happens half-way between the nut and the bridge, which is directly over the 12th fret. The 12th fret harmonic is the easiest to produce. In Figure 1, the harmonic is produced by lightly and *momentarily* (take the left-hand finger away immediately after sounding the harmonic) touching a string *directly over* the 12th fret, and by plucking that same string with a right-hand finger very near to the bridge.

Since overtones occur at regular intervals along the string (see Figure 2), the string length is the dependent variable for where the overtone exist.

Harmonics only happen at specific places along the fingerboard, as we said. In Figure 2, we see that natural harmonics may be produced at the 5th, 7th, 12th, 19th and 24th frets. Since most guitar fingerboards do not extend to a 24th fret, you might even want to put some temporary mark (tape, chalk) where the 24th fret harmonic *would* occur. To locate the 24th fret harmonic, simply measure the distance between the 12th fret and the 5th fret and then using that distance, measure from the 12th fret toward the soundhole and place the temporary mark on the guitar body. With a little more effort, you will find that harmonics may also be produced at the 3½, 4th, 9th, and 16th frets, but these produce a less distant sound, which brings us to the artificial harmonic.

Artificial Or Octave Harmonics. Because there are only a limited number of natural harmonics on the guitar's fingerboard another technique was invented to bring more harmonics to a composition. Octave, or artificial, harmonics have long been used in classical guitar music and by such contemporary artists as Chet Atkins and Roy Buchanan to widen the scope of their music. These harmonics may be obtained an octave (12 frets) above any fretted note. The idea being that you use your left-hand finger as a "nut" of the guitar and produce the harmonic by touching and picking the string with two of your right-hand fingers (see Figure 3).

In the example shown, first depress your left-hand finger on the G note at the third fret (of the low E, sixth string); next, count up 12 frets to the

15th fret, then, with your right-hand index finger, lightly touch the sixth string (low E) *directly over* the 15th fret; finally, pluck the string with your right-hand middle (second) finger and quickly remove your right-hand index finger after striking the string. Some players (Atkins among them) pick the harmonic with their thumb; others (Segovia, for example) pick it with the third finger.

Michael Brooks

Figure 3.

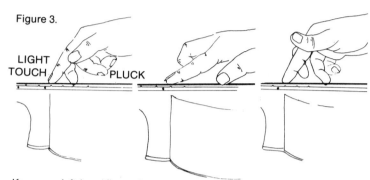

LIGHT
TOUCH   PLUCK

Keep your left-hand finger depressed on the string all through the sounding of the artificial harmonic.

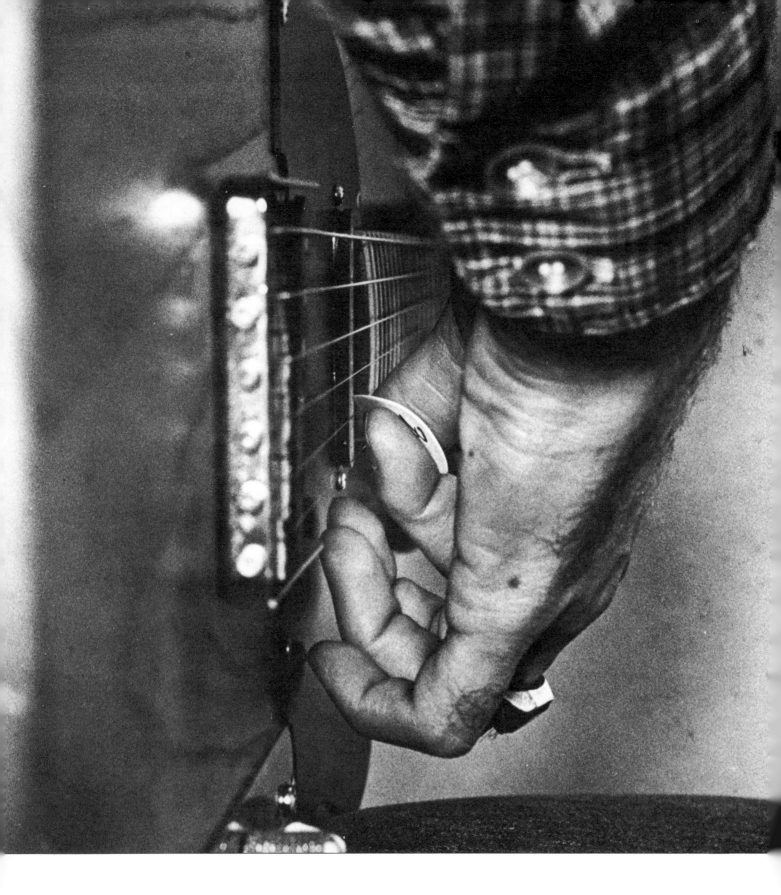

7. THE RIGHT HAND

INTRODUCTION TO PICKING

Of all the areas to be mastered, the technique of picking is the most personal and subtle, and it is an identifying factor of primary importance in creating an individual sound. The picking motion is the end result of a series of coordinated muscular movements beginning with the shoulder and ending with the tip of the pick. This is a cantilever system, with muscles pulling fingers and the bone structure of the arm supporting the muscles. This involves five separate areas: the shoulder, the elbow, the wrist, the thumb and index finger, and the tip of the pick. Movements that originate from the shoulder are large and sweeping. The elbow motion is still a sweeping movement, but it is more controlled or confined. The wrist movement is a flicking type of motion. (Rhythm playing comes from the shoulder, elbow, and wrist; single-note playing uses small, circular, scalpel movements produced by the thumb and index finger.)

The attack is achieved by the pressure point created by the thumb pushing the pick against the index finger. When the pick is held loosely it produces a loose attack. Holding the pick tightly gives you a rigid attack. This does not change the actual process of the pick contacting the string. The clarity of the sound is created by the precision with which the pick contacts the string; the quality of the attack is created by the way the pick is held. In order to achieve a good attack, a conscious effort must be made to synchronize the action of the left hand with the picking motion.

In summary, think of picking in terms of the total picture, starting from the shoulder and ending at the tip of the pick; at the same time be aware of all the various elements involved. Also keep in mind the goal of having an open-minded attitude that allows your subconscious and ears to find the best picking action.

Through the evolution of the guitar to the present time, amplification has greatly changed the picture. The guitar is now capable of achieving many different tonal colors, and the player can no longer rely on a thorough knowledge of just one or two of the elements of picking, such as using only the wrist, or the elbow and wrist, etc. Players must develop all the elements of picking. An assortment of picks should be tried as well—different sizes, shapes, and gauges— since the type of pick used is a governing factor in achieving the desired sound. With an experienced player the choice of fingerings in the left hand will greatly influence the manner in which the strings will be picked.

Wrist picking. The first area we need to develop in the picking system is the wrist. This movement has evolved from banjo players who found it necessary to play chords of three or four notes at the same time. When leaders started to use rhythm guitars in dance bands, this process continued. One of the basic needs of the orchestral guitarist of the 1930s and '40s was volume, and many solo passages played during this period used a combination of single notes and chordal-style music. The movement used for chordal-style music was very large at times, while for single-note playing it was small.

The beauty of wrist picking is the flush attack achieved by flicking the wrist, allowing the pick to enter the point of impact with the string in a perpendicular fashion. No part of the right hand touches the guitar, leaving the wrist free for this movement. For this style, keep your thumb joint flat and locked into place, and use the ball of your thumb as a pressure point to feel the vibration of the pick as it strikes the strings. The attack and point of impact are critical for a good, round sound.

Here's an exercise for holding the pick. Make a fist with your right hand, squeezing the fingers into the palm until there is a dimple along the bottom side of the hand. You should start to feel energy in the wrist and palm of the hand. Once you've done this, loosen the index finger and thumb, making them relaxed and flexible. Insert the pick between the index finger and the ball of the thumb (which is roughly midway between the thumb's joint and tip) to hold the pick against the index finger. This is

Figure 1.

Figure 2.

Figure 3.

Figure 4.

the sensitive area that will allow you to feel the pick's vibrations. If your thumb is long, an adjustment can be made by moving the index finger away so that the squeeze occurs between the ball of the thumb and the curled index finger.

Still holding the pick, double-check the flexibility of the thumb and index finger, maintaining the squeeze into the palm of the hand. Now slowly release the pressure of the fingers against the palm until you have enough space to insert a broom handle. Take the index finger of the left hand and push it against the first joint of the right-hand thumb, locking it into place. The wrist stroke does not use oscillated picking.

Here are a few exercises to help you develop your wrist movements. For the first one, hold your pick in the proper fashion, using the ball of your thumb to hold it against your index finger. While holding the guitar in its proper position, raise your forearm to chest level, so you can see the action of the wrist. Do not attempt to strike a string yet. At the pick's point of impact with the string, the wrist will be slightly bent upward. Keeping your eyes focused on your wrist and disregarding the angle of the pick for a moment, ensure that the forearm and wrist are perpendicular to the body (see Figure 1).

Flick the wrist upwards, exaggerating the movement at this time for the follow-through of the up-stroke (see Figure 2). Then return to impact position and snap the wrist downward as a follow-through for the down-stroke. Do this ten times: impact, follow-through up-stroke, impact, follow-through down-stroke (see Figure 3). Continue to do this ten more times, this time with your fingers squeezing into the palm of your picking hand. The objective is to draw energy to the wrist and palm of the hand area, not the forearm.

This next exercise is concerned with producing the sound. Hold the pick in the proper fashion, resting it in a perpendicular angle on the *D* string. There should be a slight upward bend of the wrist for the impact. The forearm may have to be adjusted slightly to achieve this (see Figure 4).

Squeeze the pick just a little. The heel of the back of the palm should be slightly above the low *E*, *A*, and *D* strings. (Note: Do not dampen the strings with the palm.) Then, with a flicking motion, push the pick across the *D* string, allowing it to rest on the *G* string. Play the musical example below, watching the right hand go through these motions. Note that you will have to lift the pick slightly over the *D* string to achieve the correct downstrokes. Check to see that the pick is perpendicular to the string as it strikes it. The right hand should be relaxed (see Example 1).

Now, using all of the above exercises*, concentrate on the squeeze of the ball of the thumb against the index finger and play the following musical example. For the *forte*, squeeze the thumb against the index finger, for the *piano*, loosen the pressure. Feel the vibration of the pick as it strikes the strings (see Example 2).

Play the musical example below while tapping the left foot. The downbeats will occur on the down pat of the foot, and the up-strokes will occur on the up pat of the foot (see Example 3).

Jimmy Stewart

Example 1.

Example 2.

Example 3.

*It is best to use a steel-string acoustic guitar for these exercises. Strive for a good, round clear sound.

Reprinted from the text in *The Howard Roberts Guitar Book* [Playback Pub., Box 4278, N. Hollywood, CA 91607].

PLAYING BACKUP

Oddly enough, the most difficult sound to master in flatpicking isn't the "fancy stuff." Rocket-fast runs, dazzling spasms of notes and flashy riffs that bring crowds to their feet can be handled by about anyone with a supple pick and plenty of practice. The difficult sound to get is the soft, listenable, rhythmic, and full-bodied brush backup.

Is Baxter dizzy? Nope. Just listen to your fastest local flatpicker and notice that he comes apart at the seams when confronted by a simple backup assignment. Banjo pickers can't follow him; singers can't hear where he's at. It takes a set of drums and a bass to cover his weakness.

Jack Elliot had the right sound—full and solid. Most flatpickers produce a backup sound like scraping the strings with a ten-penny nail. That's because most pickers think machine gun runs and dazzling breaks are where it's at, and should a soft sound be needed—simply grab an extra-thin pick and flail away. Instant "Donovan."

But if you do it properly, the backup brush can be soft and full-sounding with any thickness of pick. In fact, a thin pick has several drawbacks, the main one being the lack of "feel" and ability to maintain speed. So we ought to work on how to get a solid, musical backup style using a medium or stiff pick, without learning any bad habits.

First of all, the flat-pick should be held exactly "neutral." No tilting it toward the ceiling to get that downward drag for softness. No tilting it down toward the floor so you can tug it up and get that airy tone. This tilting up, then down produces a wiggle-waggle wrist action that slows you down and looks crummy.

Here's the secret: Instead of holding the pick firmly between your thumb and curved index finger, with even pressure mashing against the entire pick surface, roll the pressure to the back edge of the flat-pick, away from the picking tip. (See Figure 1 and Figure 2.)

This method of holding the pick at the back edge allows the tip to wobble freely, even though you brush across the strings at a right angle. The tip of the pick will naturally drag up across the strings and get that soft sound without the constant rolling of the wrist. The upward motion of the pick will also give a soft sound as the tip drags loosely across the strings. And there's plenty of pressure at the back edge of the pick, so it won't fly out of your hand. The smaller pressure area on the pick will also cut down on perspiration which makes picks spin and slide all over the place in your hand.

Now, using the forearm but keeping the wrist relatively firm, brush down over the top four strings (4, 3, 2, 1) without losing that neutral position. Then brush up. If you do it right, you'll find you won't hang up on the first string so much. That'll stop that tinny-sounding brush style, the sign of the amateur.

I'm sure any change of method is hard to accept, but the results will usually win you over. Just remember that this fuller sound is much more interesting to listen to than loud bashing and crashing. Most flat-pickers are very quiet when they play. They learn how to use a mike if they want an audience to hear. Or they turn up the knob on their electric solidbody. Let the guitar make the sound; that's what it's for—to amplify sound. Just hit the strings and make the right *kind* of sound; that's what you should worry about. Loudness is wasted effort. It's usually not creative and takes much of the concentration and energy away from producing good music. Ritchie Havens is a rare exception to this rule, but don't let his brilliance fool you. I may be wrong, but—you ain't him. Just like trying to "flat-pick" like Wes Montgomery, using a thumb. Not for mere mortals.

Probably the best example of soft-playing which I remember occurred years ago in the dressing room at the Ash Grove in Hollywood. Ed Pearl was having a reunion of Clarence and Roland White and the Kentucky Colonels. The place was packed with bluegrass and Byrds fans alike. I was in the quietest room there. Clarence was on one edge of a cot and I was on the other. The rest of the band was getting dressed or changing

Figure 1.

FLATPICK   NO PRESSURE ON PICK HERE   APPLY FIRM PRESSURE HERE

Figure 2.

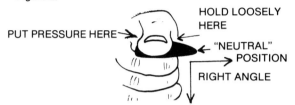

PUT PRESSURE HERE   HOLD LOOSELY HERE   "NEUTRAL" POSITION   RIGHT ANGLE

strings. After about half an hour, I realized that during the whole time Clarence had been warming up blazing fiddle tunes and dreamy leads alike and I couldn't hear a note. He was playing so softly that he went unnoticed. That's control. I never forgot that ability of his. He was the greatest flat-picker of them all, and whatever he did is worth learning.

At left are a few picking patterns to work on. For 4/4 time, play the 2/4 patterns twice per measure. For 6/8 play the 3/4 patterns twice. And don't dwell on one style too much. Mix and experiment. Listen to recordings of Doc Watson, Jack Elliot and Clarence White to hear the best. Be tasteful, not loud.

Bob Baxter

CARTER-STYLE PICKING

Of all the styles of folk and country guitar, the most familiar is the one invariably called the "Carter Family Style," "the church lick," or just plain "flat pickin'." Whatever it is called, the foot-tapping **boom**-chucka, **boom**-chucka rhythm is as ubiquitous as country music itself. It can be heard from Woody Guthrie to Johnny Cash and back again, including most of the great folk and country performers in between. A good deal of its usefulness is because it can be as simple or as complicated as you want to make it.

In its most basic form, it is a cleanly picked bass note followed by a down-up chord on the high, or treble strings. The pick is held between the thumb and forefinger (not gripped too tightly). The bass note is then picked with a downward stroke, followed by a lightly brushed down-up on the top two or three strings. This should be practiced until it becomes smooth and easy, with little hunting for the bass notes and a nice light touch on the chords. (Remember—**boom**-chucka, **boom**-chucka).

A little interest can be added to this form by using some well-placed hammer-ons. Pick your bass note open (unfretted), coming down on it with a hammering motion with the appropriate finger: in this case, your middle finger. Chords can flow from one to the other by the use of bass runs, which can be used both to break up the monotony of the constant strum, and to provide a harmony line to the song you are singing.

Now if we put these techniques all together, you can attempt the old mountain ballad, "Banks Of The Ohio." After you try this, it's up to you. There are literally hundreds of songs that can be played in this style, none of them more difficult or complicated than "Banks Of The Ohio." Take it from here and see what you can do.

Happy Traum

'Banks Of The Ohio'

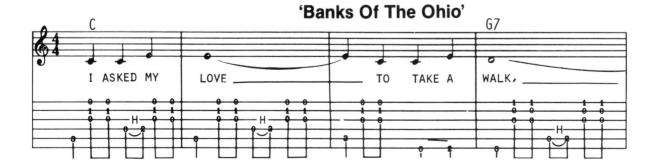

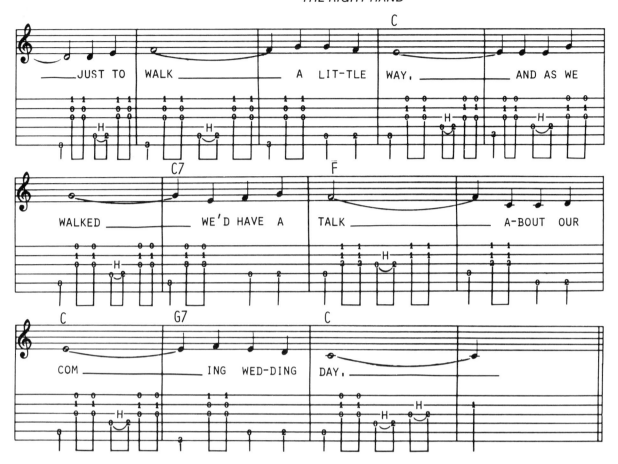

THE BLUEGRASS LICK

There's a bass run that has been used so often in bluegrass music that it has become a well-loved cliche. I call it "The Bluegrass Lick," and it often begins or ends a break, or is thrown in after a verse or a line of singing. Here it is in the five most widely used keys:

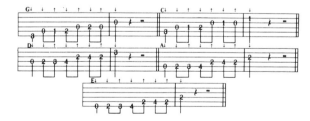

Since bluegrass guitar is usually played with a flat pick, it is important that you become facile with the pick. These runs will work as a good exercise, especially in learning to pick with alternating (down-up) strokes. Follow the arrows carefully.

Once you are familiar with the "Bluegrass Lick," try it in context by playing this instrumental I made up. I call it "The Bluegrass Breakdown."

Once you can do this smoothly, try fitting the runs into any bluegrass songs you like to sing. If you use it as an ending, the last note of the song usually corresponds to the first note of the bass run.

Happy Traum

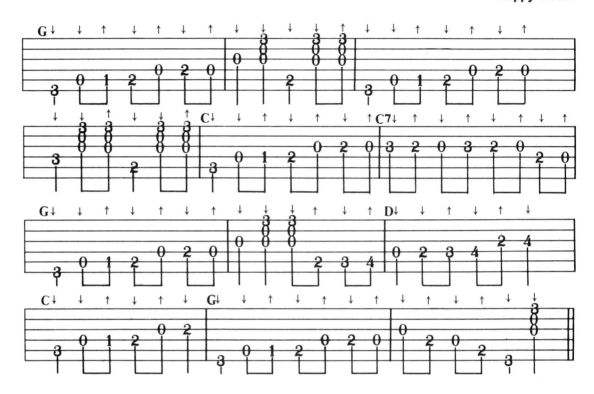

CROSS-PICKING

Cross-picking is a style of flatpicking in which the pick plays the melody note and the surrounding strings in much the same way that bluegrass banjo players do, except instead of using three fingers, the single flat pick does all the work. This means working the pick back and forth across the strings with exceptional speed and control. It usually takes a long time and a lot of practice to get it down. It should be noted that some guitarists get a similar effect by using the pick in conjunction with their second and third fingers, which means they can switch quickly from fingerpicking to flatpicking.

Here's a cross-picking version of the well-known "Dill Pickle Rag." This selection was originally a ragtime piano tune which has more recently become a virtuoso guitar/banjo/mandolin showpiece. You may hear it played in a flatpick technique on Doc Watson's *Home Again!* album (Vanguard 79239); the tune is also on the following out-of-print albums: Dave Laibman and Eric Shoenberg's *The New Ragtime Guitar* on Folkways where it is fingerpicked; on Don Reno and Red Smiley's *Another Day*, where it is played on a bluegrass banjo; and Jesse McReynolds' *Country Music and Bluegrass at Newport* on Vanguard, cross-picked on a mandolin. I used Jesse's version and turned it into a guitar instrumental which I think you will enjoy.

Before you begin "Dill Pickle Rag," it might help to practice these three exercises.

Happy Traum

CROSS-PICKING EXERCISES:

'Dill Pickle Rag,' Part I

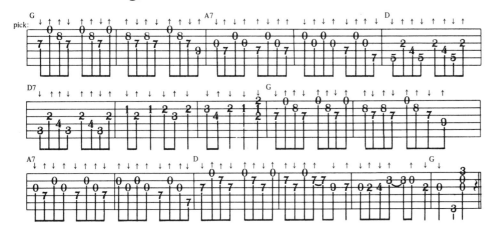

'Dill Pickle Rag,' Part II

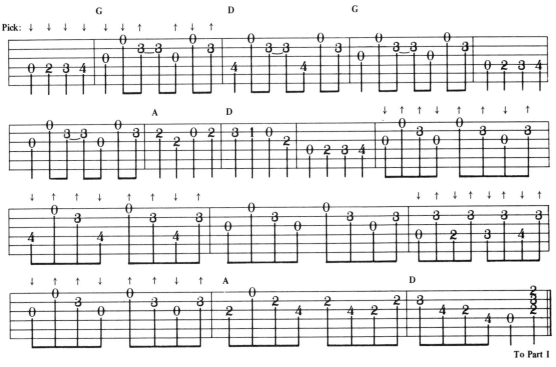

To Part I

↓ =DOWNSTROKE   ↑ =UPSTROKE

BEGINNING FINGERPICKING

Once you have strummed chords and used arpeggiated patterns with all your songs to the point of self-satisfaction, you might want to add another dimension to your playing technique. The fingerpicking style first appeared in the early 20th Century ragtime piano playing and developed with guitarists trying to mimic this sound.

Before you actually embark on the path to becoming a fingerpicking guitar player, you should first listen to some of the guitarists who are most representative of this style: Elizabeth Cotton (Folkways), John Fahey (Takoma), Stefan Grossman (Transatlantic), Mississippi John Hurt (Piedmont, Vanguard), Bert Jansch (Reprise, Vanguard), Mance Lipscomb (Arhoolie), Happy Traum (Capitol), and Mike Seeger (Vanguard, Folkways)—and these are just a few of the good examples of this style.

The style requires a *feel*, and eventually becomes less and less of a technically mental thought, and more and more of a reflex action as you develop. It is important, however, that you do listen to records of this style so that you can develop a "feel" for the music.

Step One. To master fingerpicking technique is to develop independence of the right-hand thumb in alternating-bass patterns. In fingerpicking, the thumb should learn to function, more or less, by itself, without much thought given to which string it should hit—the action should be derived more by reflex than thought after you have started. So to begin, the right-hand thumb should learn to alternate, striking the root and fifth tone of each chord. Example 1 illustrates a simple exercise for alternating, with your thumb, the root and fifth notes of various chords. While to some this thumb exercise will seem too much of a breeze to work out, you must remember that it isn't this actual exercise that will lead you on, but the *reflex* you will be developing while you work through this exercise. During the execution of this exercise, you should perhaps place your right-hand index and middle fingers on the first and second strings of the guitar, respectively. This will aid your hand in adjusting to the position required to play what is called "Three-finger picking" (thumb and two fingers).

Key of C—Alternating Bass using Right Hand Thumb.

Depending on your ability to learn, you should probably practice this exercise one hour a day for a week. Also, while you're practicing the alternate-bass, you might want to substitute different chord progressions and learn what the root and fifth notes are of the various chords in those progressions. The illustration (see Example 1) presents progressions in a few of the more common keys with the root and fifth notes of the various keys with the root and fifth notes of the various chords designated (R=root and 5=fifth).

Example 1.

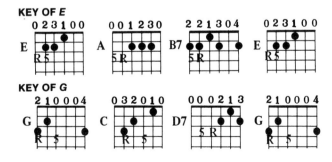

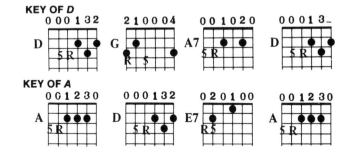

Now just substitute these progressions as they appear into the first exercise and really get that alternating thumb down. Later on you will find that your thumb automatically goes to the root and fifth of these chords without your even thinking about it.

Step 2. This calls for the use of the treble strings (the top three, *E, B,* and *G*). Here, in Example 2, is a set of exercises which should help you develop the basic technique of using alternating bass and treble strings simultaneously.

Now let's explore a few developing exercises to introduce the "syncopated" sound of fingerpicking and learn a simple song.

Syncopation. The *feeling* of fingerpicking is an alternating-bass providing the beat while the treble strings sound out the melody and a bit of the rhythm. While it depends on the tune you're doing, quite often the bass gives the impression of a tuba going through its "ump-pa, ump-pa," beat, while the treble strings are a little lighter, since they sound out the melody.

The syncopated or "off-the-beat" sound of fingerpicking is usually created by the fingers of the right hand playing the note in-between the steady, alternating bass beats sounded by the thumb. For developing good syncopation, a metronome becomes a valuable tool and is recommended.

If the music you're playing is a little too difficult, play it slowly, but in even tempo (not varying the time). As your technique improves and you feel confident playing the piece slowly, play it at a faster tempo. The exercises should come easy to you, and you should keep in mind that they are not present to test your intelligence, but to develop your reflex (see Example 3).

Keep the beat carefully by tapping your foot four times to each measure. Once you have mastered this little exercise in timing and can play it practically without thinking, try a little variety with Example 4.

Now you should be able to play an elementary song. The first step in learning a song in the fingerpicking style is to learn and know the melody. Next, you might try singing the song through with chords. Then begin to get just the bass pattern down. Look for unusual jumps in the alternating bass pattern and note the change of the bass line at each chord change. Next, learn the finger pattern (if there is one), and timing, and then add it to the bass line with the chord changes. Then put the whole works together and you've got a song.

In the arrangement of "I've Been Working On The Railroad" (see Example 5), you will note in the tabulature that stems go up and down from the notes. When the stem points down, use your thumb, and when the stem is up, use one of your first three fingers. The RH (right-hand) ring finger (third) should play every note on the top line, the RH middle finger (second) should play all notes of the second line, and your index finger should play all notes of the third line. Each line represents a string of the guitar. The numbers placed on the lines designate the position to fret that string. For example, a 3 on the second from the top line, means to depress the second (*B*) string at the third fret.

Michael Brooks

Example 2.

Example 3.

Example 4.

Example 5.

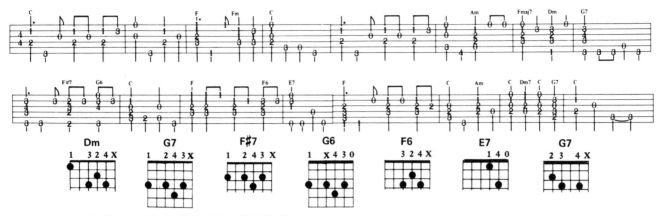

This transcription reprinted from *Easy Chord Solos for Guitar*, by Ralph Higgins.
Copyright © 1973, Belwin-Mills Publishing Corp., Melville, New York. Used by permission.

FINGERPICKING *COCAINE*

There are many versions of this song, but probably the most popular was the one recorded some years ago by Dave VanRonk, who learned it (I think) from Rev. Gary Davis. The tune has endless possibilities for improvisation, even within the rather formalized fingerpicking arrangement, and it is fun to play. It is also a plaintive, haunting song, with its refrain after each couplet, "Cocaine, all 'round my brain."

Here are two variations on the first part on the song, complete with some tricky hammer-ons, pull-offs, and moving bass lines. It shouldn't be too difficult, as long as you maintain a rock-steady bass with your thumb, and pick clean sharp treble notes with your index and middle fingers.

PART ONE

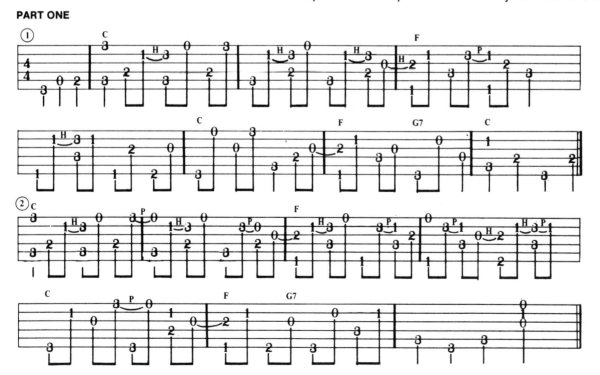

Part Two is very similar to Part One in that it entails a good deal of hammering-on and pulling off on the treble while maintaining a steady, alternating bass accompaniment (played with the thumb).

The major difference in Part Two is that the first two measures are *E7* rather than *C*. This part of the song is usually sung as a chorus, after two verses of part one. Once you have mastered these variations, try to change some notes around yourself, improvising your own version of the song.

Happy Traum

PART TWO

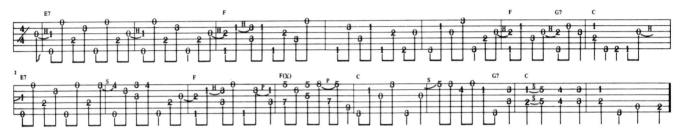

1. Yonder comes my baby all dressed in blue,

   Oh sweet mama what you gonna do?

   Cocaine, all 'round my brain.

2. Yonder comes my baby all dressed in red,

   Cocaine all around her head,

   Cocaine, all 'round my brain.

Chorus:

   Oh mama, come here quick,

   This old coke is gonna make me sick,

   Cocaine, all 'round my brain.

3. Walkin' down Fifth Street, comin' up Main

   Lookin' for a woman, gonna buy cocaine, etc.

4. Coke's for horses, not for men,

   Doctor says it's gonna kill me but he won't say when, etc.

   (chorus)

FINGERPICKING IN OPEN TUNINGS

Open tunings are valuable to know for many reasons, not the least of which is the fact that they free you from constantly having to hold down a chord. This gives you much more mobility in improvising while maintaining the steady, alternating bass that is the keystone of the fingerpicking style. If you are interested in slide (or knife) guitar, you will find it very helpful to play in an open tuning.

This version of John Henry is similar to the one played by Etta Baker on Tradition Record's *Instrumental Music of the Southern Appalachians*, and transcribed in my book, *Fingerpicking Styles for Guitar* (Oak Publications, N.Y.).

If you are just learning to pick, be sure that your thumb is keeping a steady, even beat throughout, regardless of what your fingers are doing in the treble. Once you get hold of this, try improvising variations. Don't play it the same way twice.

Happy Traum

'JOHN HENRY'   Tune your guitar to *D, A, D, F♯, A, D.*

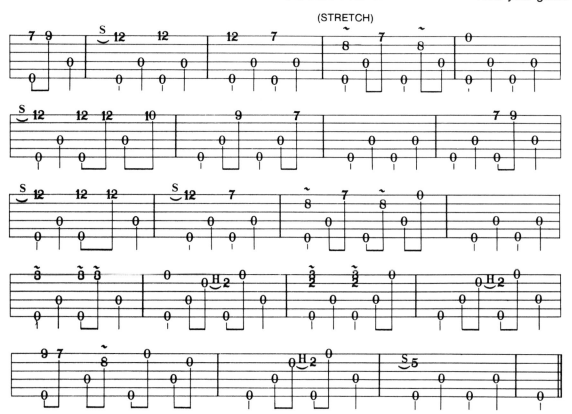

FINGERPICKING BACKUPS

Here is the key to sounding great when you play fingerpicking backups.

We all know that fingerpicking has four beats a measure played by the thumb as in Example 1.

We all know that treble strings note (played with the index or middle fingers) can play on the beat (see Example 2) or off the beat (see Example 3).

The fingers can even play these melody and counter-melody notes on *and* off the beat to create some dynamic effects (see Example 4).

But unless you have played the style for years, the even, solid, full, and rhythmic fingerpicking backup never sounds as smooth as Gordon Lightfoot's, or Dylan's, or Peter, Paul & Mary's. You know terrific-sounding fingerpicking without melody. Here's the trick. I just figured it out, actually, with students at my school. We all do it a new, simple, great-sounding way that you can master in five minutes. Simply set up the bass line shown in Example 5.

Now play the third string with the index finger and the second string with the middle finger (for smoothness) and try Example 6.

In chords that feature first-string interest, like a G to G7 change, try the same pattern, only play with the index finger on the second string and middle finger on the first string (see Example 7).

You have the same physical pattern of "beat-and-beat-and-beat-and-beat-and," but you can play on either the third and second strings or the second and first strings. Bass notes are physically played alike, but in *A*, *B*, *C*, and *D* chords play a 5 4 5 4 bass line. In *E*, *F*, and *G* play a 6 4 6 4 bass line.

Very easy. Not even a pause or syncopated silence to learn in order to make the pattern bump and tumble. Here's the point: by learning just this one style, you're going to be fantastic and solid in no time. You will get plenty of interest without having to change from complex pattern to complex pattern to achieve it. The normal changing from chord to chord will give plenty of interest and break the monotony, because each features different relationships of notes, making the pattern sound fresh each change. The easy pattern will also give you confidence to try better-sounding bass lines that are usually difficult to play while picking hard patterns. For example, you can alternate 5 4 6 4 in a *C* chord (see Example 8), or you can try a sixth string in *D* and *F* (see Example 9).

Maybe even an added finger in *G7* as in Example 10.

Listen carefully to each chord as you work out the alternating, constant bass line. You'll always discover new music.

A few other tips: Fret the bass notes cleanly so as not to cause any buzzing and thumping. Don't play too loud and make strings buzz. The guitar is a box with wires stretched over the metal frets. It's gonna buzz. If you pluck downward toward the floor with a petting motion of your thumb, instead of banging and shoving your thumb into the guitar face to make it vibrate against the fret wire, you'll get a cleaner sound. The strings should be plucked to vibrate horizontally in relation to the guitar face, not vertically against it. Takes practice.

Bob Baxter

Example 1.

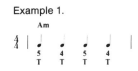

Example 2.

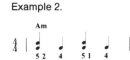

Example 3.

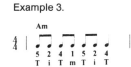

Example 4.

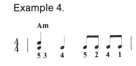

Example 5.

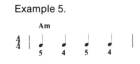

Example 6.

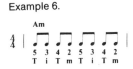

Example 7.

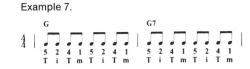

Example 8.

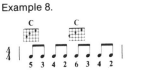

Example 9.

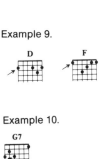

Example 10.

PLAYING ARPEGGIOS

Besides strumming the individual notes of a melody, the right hand may also be called upon to pluck the separate notes of a chord. The characteristically beautiful sound of the guitar is enhanced when the fingers of the right hand strike these notes in various patterns. The resulting arrays of notes are known as *arpeggios* (derived from the Italian word, *arpa*, which means "harp"—an instrument often associated with the image of strings being plucked individually, producing a beautiful effect). There are as many arpeggio patterns as there are sequences and combinations of strings which can be played with the right hand.

Arpeggios sound equally good on nylon- and steel-string guitars. To get a good, clear sound out of either of these instruments, you will need fingernails of moderate length on your plucking fingers. While it is the fleshy tips of the fingers that initially come into contact with the strings, the fingernails serve as a sort of backup—giving an extra edge to the sound.

Let's see how you would play a basic arpeggio in 4/4 time. First, finger a *D* chord. Play Example 1—a simple four-beat thumb/finger strum. (The thumb strikes the bass note, followed by the first, second, and third fingers plucking up on the third, second, and first [*G, B, E*] strings respectively.)

Example 1.

Now subdivide the last two quarter notes of each measure into four eighth-notes, using the first, second, and third fingers as shown. Make sure that the timing is accurate, the "three-and-four-and" of the arpeggio takes the same time to play as the "one, two" in the first part of the measure (see Example 2).

Example 2.

Example 3.   Example 3 is a song to use when practicing this arpeggio technique.

As we have seen, playing arpeggios involves the subdivision of the beat into smaller parts. We divide or subdivide the notes of the basic three- or four-beat measure into smaller units (such as eighth-notes), and when the patterns are superimposed on the notes of a chord, the result is an arpeggio. In 3/4 time, this subdivision will give us six eighth-notes per measure. Since we normally use the thumb and the first three fingers of the right hand to play arpeggios, two of the fingers must be used twice in order to arrive at six notes.

In Example 4, it will be the 1st and 2nd fingers (index and middle, respectively) that will do double duty. Finger a *C* chord, and play the basic three-beat, bass/chord strum.

Example 4.

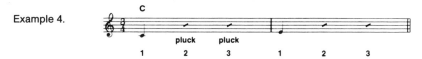

Now, let's subdivide all three quarter notes of each measure so that we have an arpeggio of six eighth-notes. Be sure that your timing is accurate (play the notes evenly). If you play the example correctly, the "one-and, two-and" of the eighth-notes should be of a duration equal to the "one, two" of the quarter notes (see Examples 5 and 6).

Example 5.

Example 6.

Some songs or parts of songs sound best when an all-arpeggio pattern is used. In these instances, just play an endless stream of eighth-notes. You might want to add some bass notes occasionally to help break up the constant flow and therefore add interest. Here is an example of a song in 3/4 time that illustrates the different effects of alternating (1) mixtures of arpeggios play "one, two, three" patterns and (2) an all-arpeggio pattern (see Example 7).

Jerry Silverman

Example 7.

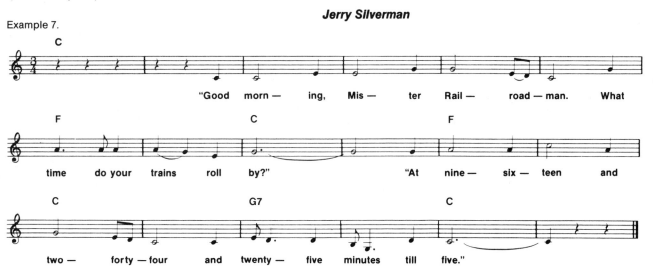

"Good morn — ing, Mis — ter Rail — road — man. What time do your trains roll by?" "At nine — six — teen and two — forty — four and twenty — five minutes till five."

8. LEAD GUITAR

LISTEN FOR THE LEAD

Example 1.

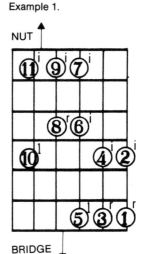

One of the most helpful ways for any guitarist to learn and expand, is by listening to good albums. Although this method is hardly new to guitarists, there are some problems which beginning players encounter when they attempt to decipher the styles and techniques of guitarists on record. Sometimes the mixing of the album itself confuses and obscures the sound of the guitar, other times a heavy background (bass, drums, brass section or whatever) will cover up the sound of the guitar; furthermore, sometimes the ear of the listener is not attuned to picking out the guitar. Blues and country albums are probably the easiest to begin learning from as they usually provide more than enough volume to the lead guitar, and there are seldom over-dubs obscuring the technique.

Usually, the best method to start with is to pick the first note of the album out and try to find it on the high *E* string. Once this is accomplished, and you know a little about lead guitar patterns, you can easily play along for a bit with the lead instrument. One lead pattern that is most easy to identify and play along with is found in the example below. This one is easily found in John Mayall's album, *Turning Point*, the cut "Roxanne." Also, this particular example is in harmony with Creedence Clearwater's "Keep on Chooglin!" To play this pattern with these cuts, merely match your starting note on the high *E* string with the starting note on the album, and then follow through. Don't be limited by this pattern, however. Experiment with notes around it.

If you don't happen to have these records around, you can have a friend play the music below (see Example 2), while you play through this lead pattern. In the music below, your friend will simply play the basic chords, four beats to a measure, while you run through the lead (see Example 1). The large numbers which are encircled represent the sequence of the lead pattern, while the small letters represent the fingers used (i = index, m = middle, r = ring, and l = little finger).

In order to play this pattern, you must strike only the string your left fingers are depressing on the fingerboard. As far as the tempo, you should use your own discretion, but the first couple of times through the music you should probably play at a moderately slow pace. Begin this pattern on the high *E* string, play a high *E* (the thinnest string) at the twelfth fret. Enjoy yourselves!

Michael Brooks

Example 2.

MOVABLE LEAD PATTERNS

Just as there are movable *chords* for the instrument, there are also movable *lead patterns* which designate the notes played in any particular key. The following are two movable patterns which many guitarists have found significant in establishing the basis for lead guitar breaks and fill-ins, especially in the musical fields of blues and rock. You should view these patterns (see Examples 1 and 2) not only as whole runs, but also view parts of them as short runs or fill-ins. You should also attempt to experiment around with these patterns and look for "notes which may be added to these patterns" which will blend tonally as well as artistically to the piece of music you are playing.

In the long run, the most efficient left hand fingering (reverse for left-handed guitarists playing left-handed) is that shown by the numbers placed next to the notes on the fingerboard diagrams (see Examples 1 and 2). Also, you should try to work through these patterns with consecutive up-and-down strokes for right-hand picking.

Selecting the proper pattern and its placement on the fingerboard is done quite easily. In each pattern, you will note (again, see Examples 1 and 2) that on one particular fret, the notes to be depressed (designated by the circles) run consecutively across the fingerboard. This for clarification, will be called the KEY FRET. So that the Key Fret is that which contains all the notes depressed across the fingerboard. If you look at the table below (see Example 3), you will notice that for each fret, a specific key is indicated.

If you are to play a song, like Creedence Clearwater's "Keep On Chooglin'" which is in the key of *E*, looking at the table (Example 3), you will see that the pattern in the key of *E* is located at the 12th fret. So the Key Fret is the 12th and you can then begin playing either pattern just so long as the Key Fret is lined up on the 12th fret. If one pattern doesn't seem to work, use the other. Also, in some songs, you can combine both patterns (see Example 4) like in the example given below in the key of *E*.

Not by any stretch of the imagination should this article be considered a thorough explanation of the full value of lead patterns. It is merely a quick, easy introduction into lead playing, which we felt might be helpful. It still remains that the best method is a strong music theory course supplemented by listening to the lead of your favorite guitarists, but interpret, try not to copy.

Michael Brooks

Example 1.　　　　　　　NUT ↑

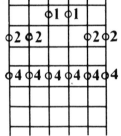

Example 2.　　　　　　　NUT ↑

Example 3. *Key Fret Table.*

FRET NO.	1	2	3	4	5	6	7	8	9	10	11	12	13	14	15	16	17	18	19	20
KEY	F	Gb	G	Ab	A	Bb	B	C	Db	D	Eb	E	F	Gb	G	Ab	A	Bb	B	C

Example 4.

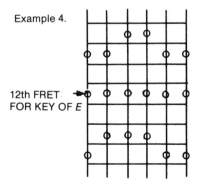

12th FRET
FOR KEY OF *E*

9. THE BLUES

BLUES PROGRESSIONS

The standard 12-bar blues progression is the single form which is used most in popular music today. And while many hundreds of songs have been written using the same basic progressions, thousands more exist containing variations of the pattern. The single piece of material called blues is so malleable, and has therefore been so widely adopted, and adapted, that an understanding of popular music is impossible without a knowledge of how a blues progression can be used.

In its standard form, the blues progression consists of three phrases, each four bars long. The first phrase is entirely on the tonic, or key, chord (*C*, for example. All the sample progressions given here have been transposed to *C* for easy comparison). The second phrase is divided between the subdominant and tonic chords (two bars of *F* followed by two of *C*). The last phrase contains one bar of dominant (*G*), one bar of subdominant, and two of tonic. Thus: *C, C, C, C/ F, F, C, C,/ G, F, C, C.* Alternatively, the first phrase may appear as: *C, F, C, C.* At the end of the thirds phrase, a "turnaround" is optional. The standard form of this transforms the third phrase into: *G, F, CF, CG*; (two letters occuring together mean that each chord is played during *half* the bar.

In addition, 7ths may be added to most triads below. Also, some passing chords have been omitted for simplicity.

Altering the Blues.
1. The dominant and subdominant chords may be replaced by other chords, Here is the Grateful Dead's "Cumberland Blues": *C, C, C, C/ C, C, C, C/ B, D♯E, D♯, C.* Or consider Hot Tuna's "Easy Rider Blues" (all the Hot Tuna examples given here are from their first album, a record which contains a wealth of variations on blues progressions): *C, B♭F, C, C/ C, B♭F, C, C/ E♭B♭, E♭G, C, C.*

2. One phrase may be in a different key than the others. Here is Hot Tuna's "Hesitation Blues": *AmE, AmE, AmE, AmC7/ F, F, C, C/ G, G, CF, CG.*

3. The 12-bar progression may be extended to 16 bars by lengthening the third phrase so that it becomes a chorus (the lyric sung over it being the same in every verse). Here is Hot Tuna's "Search My Heart": *C, C, C, C/ F, A♭, C, C/ C, C, C, C/ F, G, C, C.* The first two phrases are of normal construction, but the third is extended so that it becomes two phrases. Hot Tuna's "Death Don't Have No Mercy," is also of this form; *Cm, FmG, Cm, Cm/ Cm, B♭, E♭, G/ Cm, Cm, Fm, Fm/ CmE♭, FmG, Cm, Cm.*

4. The progression may also be lengthened to 16 bars by doubling the length of the first phrase, so that the last two become the chorus. Normally, four vocal lines, each two bars in length, will then be sung over the first phrase. Here is "Walkin' the Dog," from Redwing's album *What This Country Needs . . .* : *C, C, C, C, C, C, C, C/ F, F, C, C/ G, F, C, G.*

5. A progression using the circle of 5ths may be introduced into the blues pattern. For instance: *C, F, C, C/ F, F, C, A7/ D7, G7, C, C.* Or, in the 16-bar pattern given above, the circle of 5ths might be used as follows: *C, F, C, C/ C, F, E7, E7/ A7, A7, D7, Fm/ C, G, C, C.* In Hot Tuna's "Winnin' Boy," the following occurs: *G, G, CF, C/ G, G, C, E7/ A7, A7, Dm, DmD7/ G, G, CF, C.*

6. The progression may be lengthened asymmetrically, or occur in combined forms. Redwing's "Baby C'mon," from the same album, contains the following 14-bar progression: *C, C, C, C/ F, F, C, C/ G, F, E♭, F, C, C.* In "Soul Theft," also from the same album, the first verse is a shortened blues progression: *C, C, C, C/ B♭, F, C, C.* The second verse is a different progression lengthened by adding one

bar to the middle of the third phrase and two to the end: *C, C, C, C/ G, G, G, C/F, A♭, B♭, C, C, C, C*. Finally, the two progressions are combined into a single 19-bar progression, thus: *C, C, C, C/ B♭, F, C, C/ G, G, G, C/F, A♭, B♭, C, C, C, C*.

The involved chord substitutions used by jazz blues players are beyond the scope of this column. But even without getting into them, the reader should be able to see that the possibilities offered by blues progressions are endless. By using some of these variations, musicians can explore many of the subtle effects offered by harmonic change, without for a moment losing the emotional directness that comes from the fact that they're just playin' the blues.

Jim Aikin

THE BLUES: AN IMPROVISOR'S BEST FRIEND

Your basic beginning guitarist watches a professional axe-slinger jamming and blowing away, improvising and effortlessly composing on the spot, flying soulfully and skillfully by the seat of his pants, as it were, and exclaims, "How the hell does he *do* that?" Well, if you break it right down and analyze it, the basis for improvisation in almost any form or style of today's western music comes from a thorough knowledge of, and a sympathetic feel for, the blues.

The theory behind traditonal blues goes something like this (this is to show you that I know what I'm talking about, so please read the following in a subdued, scholarly tone): The blues is a harmonic structure extending 12 bars (measures), containing a progression consisting of the three basic chords (tonic, subdominant, and dominant), with a melody or improvisational solo based on the blues scale (root, ♭3, 4, ♭5, 5, ♭7, octave). Then you throw in the magic ingredient — what I'll call personality; what my friend the teacher calls creativity, inspiration and (above all) courage; but what B.B. might refer to as blood, sweat, and tears of heart and soul.

Now for those of you in need of a translation of all the above . . . A verse of standard blues song *usually* lasts 12 bars, which is 48 beats, or foot taps. In one of its simplest forms, those 12 bars have three chords that follow the order shown in Example 1. Don't let the Roman numerals throw you. This is just my way of giving you a theory lesson—which everybody usually fears and hates, because it's egghead stuff and not as much fun as learning the changes to last week's hit, or copping the solo off the record. Well, surprise, surprise! You'll be amazed at how much faster and easier it is to cover new material when you understand the how-what-why-and-where of it all.

You see, in theory, you take an ordinary major scale (known in academic circles as the *ionian* mode), and then give each "degree" of the scale a number. For example, the C major scale goes like this: *C*-I, *D*-II, *E*-III, *F*-IV, *G*-V, *A*-VI, *B*-VII. Then, using only notes found in that scale, you build chords on each scale degree. So that stuff you learned in grade school about do, re, mi, etc. (that name-calling is *solfeggio*, by the way, but I'm sure you all know that), which later in practical application became a limited alphabet (*A* to *G*, sharped or flatted, repeating ad infinitum), now enters *another* parallel universe called theory—where the chords that are built on those aforementioned scale degrees simply get the same corresponding numbers. (Whew! Okay, now go back and slowly read this paragraph once more, skipping all the junk in the parentheses, and you'll have absorbed your first theory lesson, you brown-noser, you.)

Example 2 shows that three-chord 12-bar progression in C. For variations, you could substitute some funky dominant 7th chords for the majors in any of these progressions, or if you're really sad and low-down, you could play all the changes as minor chords for a whole new mood and sound.

Let me impress upon you the elements of this structure that should come naturally, which you'll eventually develop an instinct about: the move up to the IV chord in the fifth bar, then return to the root chord in the seventh bar; and the move to the V chord in the ninth bar, and the gradual return to the root chord in the 11th bar *through* the IV chord in the 10th bar. The last two bars are called the *turnaround*, the musical place that ties off the 12-bar package and returns you to the top to start all over. There are hundreds of variations that exist for turnarounds, but a unique statement in the 12th bar is an important compositional aspect of 12-bar blues. Some good examples of 12-bar song structures are: "I Can't Quit You, Baby" by Led Zeppelin (a slow blues with a unique turnaround), "Thrill Is Gone" by B.B. King (down-tempo with minor chord changes, "Tush" by ZZ Top (a shuffle feel), and "Mercury Blues" by David Lindley (with a straight-eight rock and roll feel and a slightly altered chord structure—instead of V, IV, I, its last four bars go VIm, V, I).

Rik Emmett

Example 1.

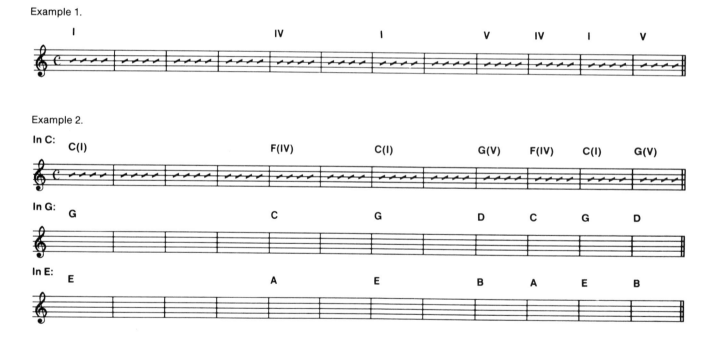

Example 2.

IMPROVISING WITH THE BLUES SCALE

Building a strong foundation for improvising involves becoming familiar with the blues scale. Example 1 shows what the blues scale looks like in *E* (zeroes denote open strings):

Example 1.

Look at Example 2 to see the same scale in *A*.

Example 2.

Try to develop your 4th finger so you'll have good positional technique, a building block for the future.

In the same way that you have to feel for the changes in a 12-bar progression (memorized to the point of pure instinct, like breathing in your sleep), you've got to know this scale intimately, in many positions with infinite variations, to become a skilled improviser.

One of the first position-shifting variations of the scale that I learned appears in Example 3.

Example 3.

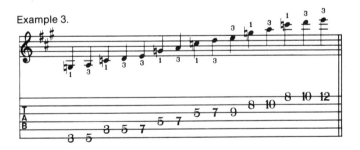
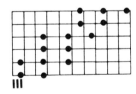

To be 100% accurate, the actual notes shown in the last example are the notes of a *C* pentatonic (five-note) scale, which I suppose you could say gave birth to the *A* blues scale—adding through evolutionary genetic mutation that weirdo extra note, the flat 5.

When it comes to soloing, improvising, and composing, the blues is the style and state of mind where almost all modern guitarists (legends, rock stars, columnists, even the Next New Thing) started, and it's where they return again and again. It is basic, simple, and direct, but it's the very honest, pure lifeblood of American music. So get directly down, gentle reader, and start learning to fly by the seat of your pants.

Rik Emmett

BLUES INTRODUCTIONS

One sign of an accomplished guitarist is his use of embellishments in his music. Usually these little indications of professionalism are found in introductions and endings; these are very effective one- or two-measure musical passages which are easy to play, even for the novice.

The most important ingredient in playing introductions is *feeling*, for it is feeling that founded the blues. It is very easy to play these little passages with *no* feeling at all, but that's just how it will sound—no feeling. Playing with feeling is an abstract emotional approach which you will gradually master as you listen to more and more music. In a strictly musical sense, the terminology of feeling finds expression through dynamics: Playing passages softly and delicately or harshly and loud, depending on the effect desired and the mood one wishes to convey.

Attempt these blues introductions using both loud and soft volume, and as much feeling as you can put into them.

Introductions In The Key Of *E*. The introductions here are typical for the key of *E* blues, but it never seems to get boring. (See Introductions 1, 2, and 3.)

Introductions In The Key Of *A*. Here are three more introductions, but these are in *A* (see Introductions 4, 5, and 6). You might want to transpose some of the key of *E* introductions above into the key of *A*. The most common blues keys are *E, A, D,* and *G.* In Introduction 5, you might find it easier to begin with the little finger (left hand) for the fourth-string (*D*) tones. This way you won't have to stretch your second and third fingers beyond repair. Good Blues!

Michael Brooks

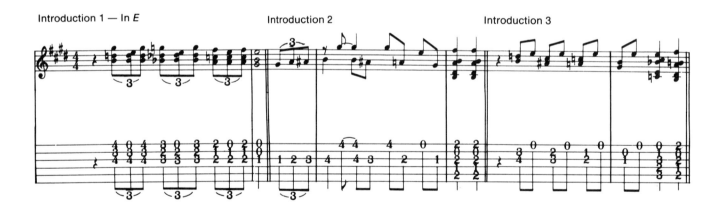

Introduction 1 — In *E*   Introduction 2   Introduction 3

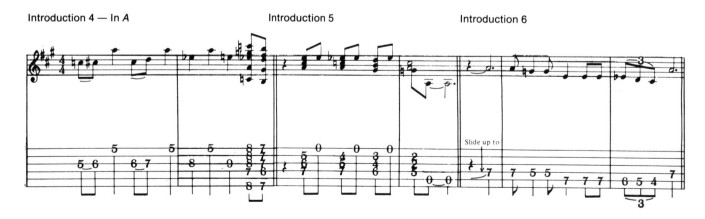

Introduction 4 — In *A*   Introduction 5   Introduction 6

PLAYING BLUES BREAKS

One of the major characteristics of a blues song is the pause in the vocal part between phrases. For instance, if the stanza is three lines long and consists of 12 measures of music, the chances are that only about six of those bars will be sung. The pauses in the singing generally occur two measures at a time—at the end of the first, second, and third lines, respectively (that is, at bars 3 and 4, 7 and 8, 11 and 12).

When the voice is actually singing, the guitar may content itself with "merely" playing the accompaniment. But during those two-measure pauses, it is virtually incumbent upon the guitarist to fill-in with meaning-ful instrumental passages, or "breaks," as they are often called.

Example 1 shows where the breaks fall in a typical three-line, 12-bar blues. It is obvious from this example that in any typical blues verse the guitar must solo about half the time.

Example 1.

The break serves a dual function: First, during the moments of vocal rest, it acts as a filler to keep things moving; and secondly, it acts as a harmonic and melodic bridge between the chords on either side of it. It therefore follows that the breaks listed as I, II, and III should be different in their harmonic and melodic makeup, since they link different pairs of chords. (Break III is, of course, none other than the blues ending that we discussed previously.)

How does an aspiring blues guitarist get inspiration to play the proper breaks? Where do all those great ideas come from? Primarily from the melody of the song itself. So, the first thing you have to do is play the particular melody you're working on (but not while singing it) until it really sticks with you. Hopefully, you'll remember little fragments of each subsequent melody you learn and be able to use them as the basis for your future blues breaks and variations. As there is often similarity in blues melodies, certain instrumental as well as vocal passages do recur often enough for them to be thought of as standard. So eventually, you will be able to build up a whole array of possible fills, though nobody ever said it's easy!

Shown are some examples of breaks I, II, and III in the key of C that you may fit into this song and other blues in C.

Break I

Break II

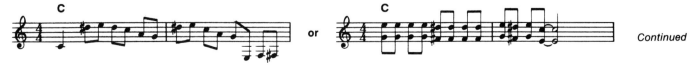

Continued

Break III

or

Here are some characteristic breaks in *G, D, A,* and *E.*

Jerry Silverman

BOTTLENECK/SLIDE GUITAR BASICS

Bottleneck/slide guitar is probably the most exciting technique that an acoustic or electric guitarist can use. The effect of a glass bottle's neck, metal tube, or even a knife blade on the strings produces an incredible array of sounds—from the cry of the blues to the calm of a hurricane's eye.

Duane Allman took this technique into the realms of popular rock, playing strong, melodic lines on his electric in a band context. While his musical ideas were quite original, their roots could still be traced to various influences. In and around the Mississippi delta, bluesmen during the first part of the twentieth century experimented and recorded with bottleneck/slides: Son House, Hambone Willie Newburn, and Robert Johnson were among those who created important blues performances using this technique. (Fred McDowell continued the tradition in the early '60s, though his style varied from a rhythmic lick approach to one capturing a melodic line.)

Acoustic blues played with the bottleneck traveled up the Mississippi to Chicago in the '40s, where guitarists such as Muddy Waters amplified an instrument, doing the same arrangements on electric that he had done previously on acoustic. Elmore James took Robert Johnson-inspired licks and placed them in the forefront of his band. Johnson's "Dust My Broom" has become a standard, and the trademark of the tune is its opening slide passage.

Since the most difficult technical aspect of this approach is the control you will need to develop with the slide, let's immediately get down to basics. The type of bottleneck/slide you use will determine the quality of sound you achieve. For example, although a glass bottleneck will produce a certain sound, it also can vary depending on the glass' weight. Similarly, a heavy metal tube produces a different texture than, say, a thin copper lipstick holder. I have even heard of animal bone being used. Again, the weight of the bone is very important to the texture of the sound produced. I personally use the top of a wine bottle, which is quite thick and has parallel sides. To make this slide I use the primitive approach of breaking the bottle against a curb and hoping for the best. If you want to experiment with a metal slide, you can buy a commercially made one or go to just about any hardware store and check out tubing. The store's employees might think you a little strange as you poke your fingers into the tubes, but such is life for us guitarists.

Once you've decided on the bottleneck/slide—and I suggest you try both glass and metal before coming to a final conclusion—you are ready to set up your guitar. String action should be quite high, since with a bottleneck we'll be sliding on the strings rather than pressing them down. We want to avoid fret bumping if possible, though in such styles as Fred McDowell's those buzzes are attractive, giving added texture.

The type of guitar you use is also important. The old bluesmen generally played Stellas, heavy instruments with tons of sound and high actions. A guitar with too much tone is usually not suitable for this style, since overtones can cause problems. The bottleneck will pick up lots of sounds as it slides over the strings, so a relatively dry-sounding instrument is your best bet. In today's market, this generally means a "cheap" guitar instead of high-priced one. Some bluesmen in the '30s used metal resonator instruments, although this was more for volume needed when playing on the streets than for the actual bottleneck sound. Experiment with both wood and metal guitars if you have a chance, and let your own ears decide.

String choice is directly related to the sound you're after. Many bluesmen prefer a heavy unwound third (G) string; this gives your playing a certain immediate blues feel. Other guitarists use extremely heavy-gauge strings that produce a thick, meaty sound. Still others use flat-wounds in order to eliminate noise, yet this same noisy sliding sound becomes very important to other players.

Presuming that you are now satisfied with your choice of slide, guitar, strings, and action, you're ready to put the slide on one of your fingers. My glass slide is on my little finger, while my ring finger's on the edge of it to keep it more rigid. Different people use it in different places. Bukka White had an enormous metal tube on his little finger; Son House used one on his ring finger; Fred McDowell played with an inch-long glass tube on his little finger; Sam Mitchell, one of today's finest acoustic and electric bottleneck/slide players, uses a Mighty Mite metal slide on his ring finger. I've also seen players with the slide on their index finger. Again, you will have to experiment to see which finger is most comfortable.

Producing a bottleneck sound isn't complex; the challenge is learning how to carefully control each note played. When the tab in the music indicates a fretted position, it means that your slide should be placed *directly over that fret*. The beauty of this technique resides in getting to and from each note, and what to do once you've arrived. Vibrato is a highlight of bottleneck playing and can occur either before or after the note is slid into its fretted position. (Vibrato is realized when the note is played, and then the slide moves back and forth over that position.) Even the amount of sliding motion you employ will yield a specific sound, which can be wide or narrow. If you shake your hand in a wide arcing motion tight and close, the vibrato will reflect that movement.

There are, of course, many variables to bottleneck/slide playing. I have tried to mention as many as possible here so that you can begin experimenting with them. Enough words—let's get down to music.

Let's look at Fred McDowell's beautiful arrangement of the gospel tune "You Got To Move" (also recorded by the Rolling Stones), which can be heard on the LP *Mississippi Fred McDowell: Live In New York* [Oblivion Records, Box X, Roslyn Heights, NY 11577, od-1]. This tune's played in open *D*, tuning the strings down to *D-A-D-F♯-A-D*, low to high. Here's the best way to do it. Leave the fourth (*D*) and the fifth (*A*) strings as they are in standard tuning (*E-A-D-G-B-E*, low to high). Next, use the fourth string *D* as a guide and lower the sixth string (*E*) to match its sound to the fourth's *D*, only an octave lower. After that, lower the first string (*E*) and match its sound to the fourth, only an octave higher. Using the fifth string (*A*) as a guide to lower the second string (*B*) until it's an octave above the fifth's *A*. Finally, retune the third string (*G*) by fretting the 4th fret of the fourth string (*F♯*), and then matching that to the third string.

Tuning can be a drag, but once you've done it for a while your ears alone will be the guiding force. All the numbered tab positions here are played with the slide, and you'll be sliding up to as well as down from certain notes. The best tip I can give you at this point is to check out Fred McDowell's original version and work from there.

Stefan Grossman

'You Got To Move'　　　　By Fred McDowell

BOTTLENECK/SLIDE TECHNIQUE OF SON HOUSE

Eddie "Son" House was one of the giant bluesmen from the Mississippi Delta. He recorded a handful of sides for the Paramount Record Company in the '20s that have become blues classics. In 1942, Alan Lomax recorded Son while Lomax was on a field trip to Mississippi, and in the early '60s Son was "rediscovered" in Rochester, New York. Son's performances were fantastic, combining an energy, feeling, and musicality that are hard to describe.

I was very fortunate to be able to spend some time with Son House discussing and playing bottleneck guitar. He used two tunings for his slide pieces—open G or open D. At this time I'd like to discuss one of Son's tunes in open G called "Mississippi County Farm Blues," which is in fact an adaptation of Blind Lemon Jefferson's "One Kind Favor." There's an interesting history behind Son's writing of the song. Son told me that during the '30s when he was recording at Paramount, the news of Blind Lemon's death came in, and the producer asked Son to record a Blind Lemon tune. He took the melody from "One Kind Favor" and put his own lyrics on top. The result was "Mississippi County Farm Blues," which can be heard on the LP *Son House: The Real Delta Blues* [Blue Goose (245 Waverly Place, New York, NY 10014), 2016].

Let's talk now about the open-G tuning. It's similar to open A, except you tune the strings down instead of up. Here's how to do it: First start with your standard tuning (E, A, D, G, B, E), and then retune the first, fifth, and sixth strings. The first and sixth E's are tuned down to D. Compare these with your standard fourth D; the first should be an octave higher than the fourth, and the sixth should be an octave lower. Next, drop the fifth string A to G, matching it to the sound of the open third string G. As an extra check, once you've done all this, place your little finger on the 5th fret, first string: This will give you a G chord.

Before you play the piece, here's a suggestion: This tune has some very strong slide notes, and each fretted position in the tab should be played with your slide.

Stefan Grossman

'Mississippi County Farm Blues'   **By Son House**

Tuning: D, G, D, G, B, D

Continued

HOW I PLAY THE BLUES

Left-Hand Vibrato. I try my best to make my left hand trill evenly without any effort. For example, when I *try* to produce an even vibrato with my voice, it's very difficult, but when I just sing out naturally, the trill comes out even with no effort at all. Of course, a great deal of practice is necessary before the hand attains the dexterity required to move smoothly enough to get that vibrato. I want it just like my heart beat, something I don't have to think about at all. When I want to vary the speed of my vibrato, I try to create the same effect as when you get frightened and your heart speeds up, or when you relax and your heart slows down.

I don't trill like the average person on a violin. A violinist trills his hand from the front of the violin to the body, and most guitarists do the same thing. But my vibrato is not like that. Mine is kind of like a steady pulse, pushing the string up and pulling it down, or pushing it up and letting it go, without actually losing control of it. That's *wrong*—but it's the right way for me. All you have to do is push the string with an even flow, up and back, up and back. If you keep practicing this, finally you can control it.

When I trill I go up and down the neck instead of across the strings. There's no real explanation for this—it's just the most comfortable for me. I see some saxophone and trumpet players blow with their jaws puffed out. According to some people, that's wrong, but as someone once said about trumpeter Dizzy Gillespie, who plays with his jaw out, "There is just one Dizzy Gillespie." I didn't have any lessons in the beginning, and playing up and down the neck on trills just came natural to me.

Hand exercises. I don't use hand exercises, though I have quite a few guitarist friends who do. I've seen guys who take balls and mash them up, but I haven't found that necessary or helpful.

Equipment. I use Gibson 740 XL strings. They're an extra light gauge, but not like the slinky. I don't have any calluses on my hands at all. This is because I keep the bridge set so the strings are close to the neck. That way, I don't have to press as hard as I would on a larger gauge string.

My guitar is a Gibson ES 355. I like it because it has a long slender neck and the body balances very well. I don't use any settings, according to some people. Some guitarists, when they use the word setting, mean "Set to 1, to 5," etc. But I set my guitar according to how it sounds to me when I'm playing and I never look down to see what I'm doing. I just rotate the volume controls with my fingers, one finger moving forward or backwards against the two volume controls to make it wide open or close it.

However, I keep my amp wide open all the time. I do that so, when I need extra power, I get it from the guitar, instead of having to go to the amp and set it. The only exception is in a recording studio. Then, I record with my amp very low, never loud. But even when recording, I work my guitar settings as described above.

As most people know, my Gibson guitar is a stereo. I keep one channel closed on bass, and the treble wide open. I've got funny ears. Anything that's real bass, I can't hear very well to tell whether it's in tune or not. That's why I turn the treble up on my instrument—so I can hear better.

For amplification I use a Gibson SG system. In fact, I represent Gibson, so most of the equipment I use is theirs. Prior to that, I had a Standel, and before that the Gibson Les Paul—the Piggyback. As far as I'm concerned, the amplifier is not the most important thing. It's good as long as it amplifies the sound; that is, as long as it does what it's supposed to do. Other added features are OK and good for a lot of people, but for me, if it just amplifies, that's what I want. Of course, I turn a little bit of echo on, which enhances my music, but I don't use much—just a little.

Bending notes. When I bend notes I push up first; I never pull down. I see many younger guitarists who grab a string and pull down on it, but I never do. When bending notes, I use all my fingers, but the first three more than the little one.

My most distinctive technique. I think the best thing I've done is learning to trill in such a way that I create a sound similar to that produced by a person using a bottleneck. Trying to get that effect is what started me working on my vibrato. Also, I think I phrase a bit differently from most other guitarists. There's no real way to describe in words how I play the guitar. In order to really describe to someone how I get my sound, I'd have to show them.

B.B. King

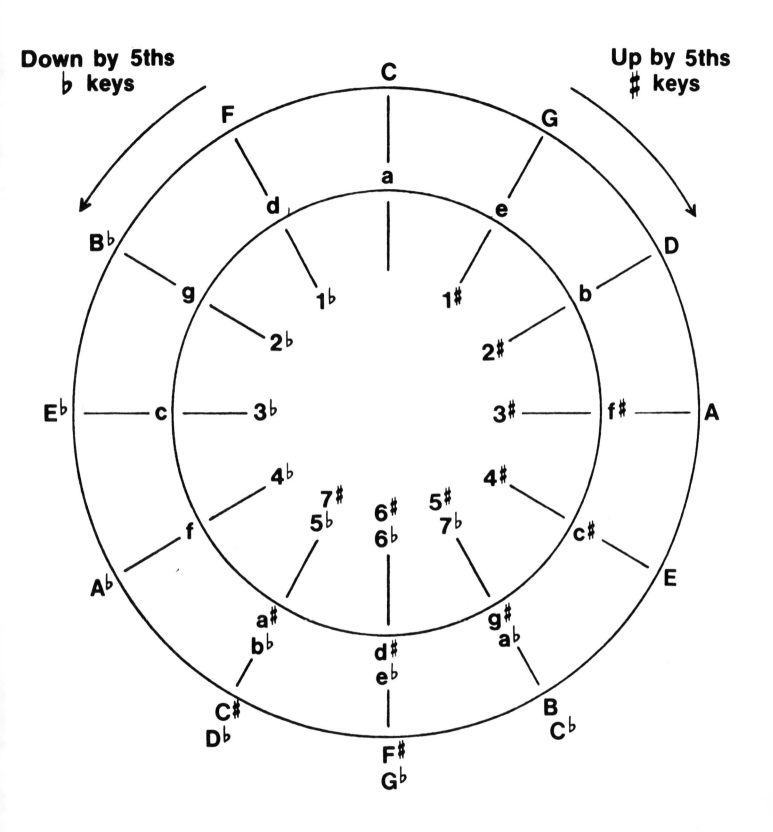

10. THEORY

THE THEORY OF MUSIC THEORY

As anyone who has ever studied music in school knows. music theory is a pivotal study—you find it as part of your course load, no matter what area of music you plan to pursue. For many people it is a vague bother; they would rather be practicing their instrument, or playing jobs at a local club, or reading obscure history texts. And if they aren't studying music in a school, but are out there trying to make it in the music business—playing guitar in a rock band, doing a lounge act, working on arrangements for some local radio commercials—then the study of theory can seem even more distant to their concerns.

So, what's the big deal? Why does everyone suggest that you learn a bunch of music theory? Why is it always a part of your course load, even if you don't plan to be a theorist? Well, it all boils down to *communication*. Understanding the fundamentals of our musical language is useful in much the same way that an understanding of English is useful—it allows you to communicate effectively.

This is not to say that people who have not studied fundamental music theory will find it impossible to make themselves understood; it's just that their music (as they write it and explain it) will have elements that will be confusing for other musicians.

For example, let us look at a common malady among musicians relative to the notation of accidentals. I have known a number of players (who knew some of the basics of notation) who used only flats and naturals in their notation—never sharps. On the surface this practice sounds straightforward and logical, but it leads to some very odd constructions, such as an *A* major triad spelled *A-Db-E*.

Now if you put that chord (spelled that way) in front of another guitar player, his or her hand will find the correct notes on the fretboard, and for that reason it may seem to be a successful way of notating that chord.

However, it will be impossible to relate that chord (spelled that way) to other elements of standard musical structure, because the underlying structure of the chord is hidden by the notation. Instead of seeing a *triad* (two superimposed thirds), you see three notes; instead of seeing the tonic chord in *A* major, you see a diminished fourth and an augmented second. In other words, the notation *A-Db-E* (if used to denote an *A* major triad) has certain pragmatic value (because it does get your hands to the correct notes), but it has no value beyond that; whereas the "correct" spelling (*A-C#-E*) has the same pragmatic value, plus a lot more. It allows you to see the structure of the chord, and relate that structure to other elements of music.

It is of course possible to come up with a number of ways to refer to or write down a particular bit of music material, and all of these ways will get the hand to the correct notes. The problem comes when you try to find the relationship between different bits of musical material. The fundamental building blocks of traditional Western music have been developed over a long period of time, and the language that we use to express these building blocks (and their relationships) has developed right along with the musical concepts. Therefore, our system of musical language and notation, if used properly, reflects the underlying structures and relationships in the music it conveys. And since those underlying structures and relationships are important to an understanding of what is really going on in music, it is very useful to master the language (because the language makes that understanding easier to come by).

By the way, I am speaking now of Western Music only. Musics of other cultures have their own theories, their own languages. Furthermore, I am speaking only *traditional* Western music theory. New developments (electronic music, microtonal music, chance music, etc.) bring with them new theories and new languages.

Knowing theory will help you in other ways, too. It's easier to memorize a piece when you can analyze its basic structures than when you're facing a mystifying storm of notes. Communicating with other musicians is easier when you can tell them exactly what you have in mind: "Give it a blues feel" is less specific than "Use a pentatonic scale."

Some people are afraid that if they learn theory, they won't be able to play as spontaneously,—and in fact, if you think of theory as a set of ironclad rules that you have to follow, it can hang up your playing (or writing). But don't let yourself be intimidated. There isn't a single theoretical "rule" that can't be broken to good musical effect. The point is to know the rules so that when you break them you'll understand what you're doing. If you understand why a certain passage sounds the way it does (maybe you're playing a *G#* dorian scale over a *Gm7♭5* chord) you'll be able to recreate the same sound later, in another tune. Knowing the theory may even suggest further possibilities to you.

So when we study music theory, we are studying an entire language and the underlying concepts of that language. It is possible to play music without ever learning a bit of theory, but theoretical understanding is a very useful tool. It allows us to see and hear relationships in the music we do, and it allows us to get those relationships in our minds and fingers. Music theory by itself won't make you understand music, but it will certainly help you to *develop* an understanding.

Tom Darter

TRIADS

In traditional harmony, chords are usually built up of superimposed thirds. A simple *C* major *triad* (so called because it contains three notes) can be found in the *C* major scale as the 1st, 3rd, and 5th notes—two thirds stacked on top of each other up from the root note, *C*. The two thirds together cover the interval of a fifth (because they overlap; see Example 1). The major triad is so named because the bottom interval (from the root to the 3rd) is a *major* third (*C* to *E*); the interval from the 3rd to the 5th (*E* to *G*) is a minor third (see Example 2).

In the minor triad the situation is reversed. In a *C* minor triad (which can be found in the *C* minor scale as the 1st, 3rd, and 5th notes), the bottom interval (*C* to *E♭*) is a *minor* third, while the interval from the 3rd to the 5th (*E♭* to *G*) is a major third (see Example 3). As with the major triad, the minor triad gets its name from the bottom interval. The interval of a fifth (*C* to *G*) that both of these chords have in common is generally called a perfect fifth.

Example 3.

If a triad is constructed with two superimposed major thirds up from *C*, the interval between the root and the 5th (*C* to *G#*) is larger than a perfect fifth and is therefore called an *augmented* fifth. The triad so formed (a *C* augmented triad) is found in the *C* whole-tone scale as the 1st, 3rd, and 5th notes (see Example 4).

Example 1.

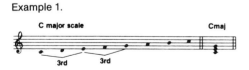

Example 2.

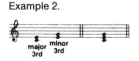

Example 4.

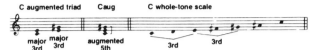

Example 5.

The diminished triad is built up of two superimposed minor thirds. It is so called because the interval from the root to the 5th (*C* to *G*♭ in the *C* diminished triad) is smaller than a perfect fifth and is therefore called a *diminished* fifth (see Example 5).

So, these are the basic forms: major triad, minor triad, augmented triad, and diminished triad. They represent all the possible combinations of two superimposed major and minor thirds. It is easy to visualize the differences in structure between these types of triads on the treble staff and the fretboard (see Example 6).

All the specific triads we have looked at so far have been in *root* position (so named because the root of the chord is also the bottom note). If we take a *C* major triad and move the root up an octave, the 3rd becomes the bottom (or bass) note. If we then move the 3rd up an octave, the 5th becomes the bottom note (see Example 7). As you can see, when we move the notes of a triad around in relation to one another, we are *inverting* the basic position of the chord. Therefore, the form of the triad with the 3rd on the bottom is called *first* inversion, and the form of the triad with the 5th on the bottom is called *second* inversion.

Of course, it is not necessary to limit yourself to these specific positions in playing a chord—any arrangement of the notes *C, E,* and *G* (in any octave) will create a *C* major triad.

It is important to realize that the sound of a chord in root position is very different than that of a chord in first or second inversion. Many different effects can be introduced through the use of different inversions and spacings in the chords you employ. This is, of course, true for all kinds of chords, from the simplest triads to the most complex six-note combinations; but the magnitude of these different effects is perhaps most clear to the ear when you are dealing with the most basic chord form—the triad. Listen to the differences between these three spacings (see Example 8).

It is a valuable exercise to experiment with triad spacings. Check out all four basic triad forms, and don't stick to just *C.* Use the whole range of your instrument. Listen carefully to the different effects you create, and remember them. They will come in handy some day. A solid understanding of triads will provide you with a firm basis for all of your harmonic explorations.

Tom Darter

Example 6.

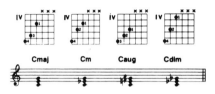

Example 7.

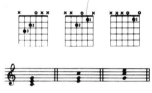

Example 8.

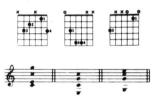

INTERVALS

In traditional theory, a chord is generally defined as a combination of three or more notes sounded simultaneously. Combinations of two notes are called intervals. The interval is the basic building block of harmony, since all types of chords can be described as combinations of intervals. (Of course, we can define a specific chord referring to the notes it contains; e.g. a *C* major chord contains the notes *C, E,* and *G.* But by using intervals, we can give a general description of every kind of chord. For example: All major triads contain three notes; there is a major third between notes one and two, and a minor third between notes two and three.) A good understanding of intervals (both aurally and visually) is therefore very important to the understanding of harmonic structure.

When we speak of a specific interval, we are simply defining the relationship between two notes in terms of the vertical distance they span. For instance, the interval from *C* up to *G* is a fifth. This is determined by counting the number of note-letters involved. From *C* to *G* includes five note-letters (*C, D, E, F, G*), so it is called a fifth.

Now, you may have noticed that the interval *C* to *G* spans more than five notes on your fretboard, and you probably also noticed that we left out certain notes by counting the note-letters (*C♯, D♯,* and *F♯,* to be exact). Why? Well, because the basic name of an interval is derived by counting the number of notes involved in the scale steps it encompasses.

So, what is a scale step? Simply a step from one note-letter to the next higher or lower note-letter. *C* to *D* is a scale step. So are *C♯* to *D* and *C* to *D♭.* Even *C♭* to *D♯* is a scale step; however, *C* to *C♯* is not a scale step. Yes, that's right: *C* to *D♭* is a scale step, but *C* to *C♯* is not. Perhaps this sounds confusing, but luckily our system of musical notation is designed to show scale steps (see Example 1). Looking at *C* to *D♭,* it's easy to see the step

Example 1

involved. *C* and *C♯* occupy the same vertical position on the staff, and so do not represent a scale step.

So it's simple. In musical notation, any move from a line to a space or a space to a line is a scale step. Therefore, in order to figure out the basic name of any interval, count the number of lines and spaces spanned by the two notes (including the lines and/or spaces occupied by the notes themselves). Going back to our first interval, *C* to *G,* it is easy to see why it is called a fifth when you refer to the lines and spaces on the staff (see Example 2). Thinking of the number of notes spanned by *C* to *G* in terms

Example 2.

of scale steps, we come up with five, and call the interval a fifth. Remember this simple rule: Count the number of lines and spaces (or the number of note-letters) to get the basic size of the interval.

But, by itself, this designation is not very exact. All of these intervals are fifths (according to the method just described), but are not all the same size (see Example 3).

Obviously, there are many kinds of fifths. We describe their different sizes in a relative way. We start with one or two basic sizes, and define the other sizes in terms of that basic form. In the case of the interval of a fifth, there is

Example 3.

one basic size: the perfect fifth (some intervals have two basic sizes: major and minor). *C* to *G* is a perfect fifth. If a fifth interval is one half-step larger than a perfect fifth, it is called an *augmented* fifth (see Example 4). If a fifth interval in one half-step smaller than a perfect fifth, it is called a diminished fifth (see Example 5).

Now that we have the basic principle down, let's go back to our collection of fifths and give them first names (see Example 6). The last two intervals here are rather unusual. The first one (*C♭* to *G♯*) is one half-step larger than an augmented fifth, so it is called a doubly-augmented fifth. The other one (*C♯* to *G♭*) is one half-step smaller than a diminished fifth, so it is called a doubly-diminished fifth.

So, we give two names to intervals. The last name (the number) gives us a basic form in terms of lines and spaces on the music staff, and the first name tells us the exact size of the interval.

Some intervals (unison, fourth, fifth, and octave) have one basic form (perfect), while other intervals (second, third, sixth, and seventh) have two basic forms (major and minor). The basic reason for this is historical. In early music, only certain intervals were considered proper for use as the final sonority in a composition. These intervals (the above-mentioned unison, fourth, fifth, and octave) were therefore called *perfect consonances*. They were pleasing to the ear, and did not require motion to any other sonority (i.e. they were completely stable). Other intervals were considered consonant in this early music (thirds and sixths), but, in terms of the musical practice at the time these intervals required resolution to the perfect consonances, and were therefore called *imperfect consonances*. The other intervals (seconds, sevenths, and all augmented and diminished intervals) were called *dissonances*; they were considered to be highly unstable, and required immediate resolution to some kind of consonance.

Even though such terms as "perfect" may have unfortunate connotations for us today, the distinctions outlined above do have a foundation in acoustics. If you examine the overtones series, you will discover that the first three intervals that occur are (in order) the octave, the perfect fifth, and the perfect fourth. In some sense, then, these intervals occur first in nature. By the way, if you want more details on the musical theory and practice discussed above, read about Medieval and Renaissance music in any music history book.

Now that we know where the term *perfect* comes from, let's go back and examine the basic forms of the intervals. An easy place to start is with the major scale. If we build intervals up from the tonic (the key note) of a major scale using only notes in the scale, we have the following scale (see Example 7).

Example 4.

Example 5.

Example 6.

Example 7.

Here we have the basic form of all of our perfect intervals; and, for those intervals with two basic forms, we have the major form. It's easy to remember: building intervals up from the tonic of a major scale gives you major seconds, thirds, sixths, and sevenths, plus the perfect intervals.

Minor intervals are one half-step smaller than major intervals. Here are the basic forms of the minor intervals (see Example 8).

Example 8.

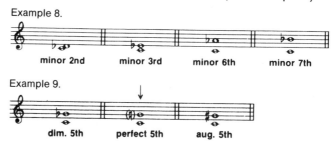

minor 2nd   minor 3rd   minor 6th   minor 7th

Example 9.

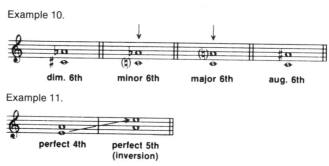

dim. 5th   perfect 5th   aug. 5th

Now that we have all of the basic forms of the intervals, we can define the other kinds of intervals in terms of their size relative to these basic forms. First, the intervals that have one basic form (perfect). If a specific interval is one half-step smaller than a perfect interval, it is called a *diminished* interval; if it is one half-step larger than a perfect interval, it is called an *augmented* interval (see Example 9).

It is easy to see that these augmented and diminished intervals are defined (and named) in terms of their relationship to the basic (perfect) form of the interval.

We see a similar kind of relationship when we look at intervals that have two basic forms (major and minor). If a specific interval is one half-step smaller than a minor interval, it is a *diminished* interval; and if a specific interval is one half-step larger than a major interval, it is an augmented interval (see Example 10).

Example 10.

dim. 6th   minor 6th   major 6th   aug. 6th

Example 11.

perfect 4th   perfect 5th
                  (inversion)

Obviously, these augmented intervals are also defined (and named) in terms of their relationships to the basic (major and minor) forms of the intervals.

Remember, the basic forms of a particular interval are always the same. Fourths always have one basic form (perfect), and thirds always have two basic forms (major and minor). There is no such thing as a major fourth, just as there is no such thing as a perfect third.

We can learn more about the relationships between various kinds of intervals by studying inversions. An interval is inverted in much the same way a triad is inverted: the bottom note is moved up an octave (and therefore the relative position of the two notes is inverted). Here is a perfect fourth and its inversion (see Example 11). There are two points of interest in this example. First, the inversion of this perfect interval is also a perfect interval; second, the interval and its inversion total up to nine. Both of these can be taken as general rules.

Now let's look at major and minor intervals, and their inversions (see Example 12).

Example 12.

Once again, the interval and its inversion total up to nine. We also discover that the inversion of a major interval is a minor interval, and vice versa.

Finally, let's consider augmented and diminished intervals (see Example 13).

Example 13.

As with all our other examples, the interval and its inversion total nine. In addition, we find that the inversion of a diminished interval is an augmented interval, and vice versa.

All of the above are general rules. The two intervals total to nine (rather than eight, the number of the octave they span) because the pivotal note is counted twice. Remember, a perfect interval always inverts to form another perfect interval, a minor interval always inverts to form a major interval, and an augmented interval inverts to form a diminished interval, and so on.

So far we have only been talking about harmonic intervals—intervals whose notes are sounded simultaneously. When the notes of an interval are sounded one after the other they form a melodic interval (see Example 14). The distinction becomes very important when we discuss inversion.

Example 14.

Harmonic inversion (the inversion of a harmonic interval) is done as described previously: the bottom note of the interval is moved up an octave, so that the relationship between the two notes in the interval is inverted. However, when inverting a melodic interval, we simply pivot the melodic shape relative to the first note, and go the same distance in the other direction (see Example 15).

Example 15.

Another detail: we have previously been concerned only with intervals of an octave or smaller—the basic forms. All intervals larger than an octave can be seen to be one of these basic intervals plus one or more octaves. For this reason, all intervals larger than an octave are called compound intervals (see Example 16).

Example 16.

For the most part, these larger intervals can be referred to as compound forms of one of the smaller intervals. However, it is possible to name them according to the same method used with the smaller intervals (by counting the total number of lines and spaces they span; see Example 17).

Example 17.

Some of these large intervals (e.g. ninths, elevenths, and thirteenths) are characteristic parts of certain complex harmonies, so it is often useful to refer to them by the larger number (i.e. major ninth rather than compound major second). The important thing is to remember the relationship that these compounds have to the basic forms—it is a relationship that is audible.

As we have said before, intervals are one of the basic building blocks of music. Obviously it would be desirable to have such a good grasp of musical notation that you could look at any interval and just *know* what it is (without having to go through any time-consuming computations). That kind of familiarity only comes with practice and use, just as it does in learning the rudiments of any language. Here is a little exercise/quiz on intervals; try to name the intervals to determine how well you are doing now (the answers are printed upside down at the bottom of this column).

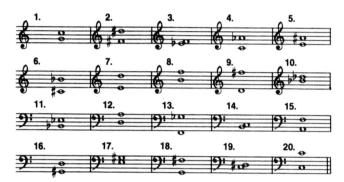

As you work on recognition of intervals, there are various methods you can use to help out. If you are familiar with scales, you can use major scales as a yardstick, by thinking of the interval's bottom note as a tonic (key note) and relating the interval's top note to the basic forms (major and perfect) formed by the tonic and the other notes of the scale (if you're not too familiar with scales yet, don't worry—we'll be getting to them). Another method involves counting the total number of semitones (half-steps) spanned by a particular interval, and relating that back to the other information you have on intervals. (For example: A perfect fifth spans seven semitones, a minor seventh spans ten semitones, and an octave spans twelve semitones. Just remember that the name of the interval does not depend on the number of semitones, but rather on the number of lines and spaces covered by the interval on a music staff.) Develop whatever methods are useful to you, and work with them (until you become so familiar with intervals that you don't need special methods any more).

Tom Darter

Answers: (1) perfect fourth. (2) major sixth. (3) major second. (4) minor sixth. (5) augmented fourth. (6) diminished seventh. (7) minor seventh. (8) diminished fifth. (9) major tenth (or compound major third). (10) minor third. (11) perfect fourth. (12) perfect fifth. (13) minor ninth (or compound minor second). (14) minor second. (15) minor sixth. (16) diminished fifth. (17) major third. (18) major seventh. (19) augmented second. (20) perfect octave.

MAJOR AND MINOR SCALES

Our term *scale* comes from the Italian *scala*, meaning "ladder." As that derivation suggests, a scale is simply an ordered progressions of pitches (usually confined within one octave) that forms the basis for certain kinds of music structure.

Scales are usually thought of as being constructed upon a particular note, which is referred to as the tonic or key note of the scale. From the tonic, the scale progresses up by scale steps (usually) until it reaches the tonic an octave higher, and then descends via the same (or similar) route to the first tonic.

In traditional tonal music (music in a particular key) the most common scale forms are major and minor. In fact, major and minor scales are much more than successions of notes that beginning guitar and piano students have practiced all the time. They provide the basic materials for (and delineate the structural hierarchies of) tonal music. For this reason, the distinction between scales and modes is important. The church modes (see your music history book—more on them later) provided pitch materials on which melodic and contrapuntal structures were based. With major and minor scales, however, another dimension was added. Although the major and minor scales that form the basis of tonal music were derived from the church modes, the entire musical practice that developed along with scales concerned itself with a massive structure of melodic and *harmonic* patterns, all of which worked toward the establishment of a particular key center (the tonic of the scale). The basic structure of tonality is implied in the structure of major and minor scales, which makes it useful to understand how major and minor scales are constructed.

First let's look at the major scales. Here is *C* major (see Example 1). Notice that there are half-steps between notes 3-4 and 7-8, while the other notes are connected by whole-steps. This is the structure of the major scale. Although a major scale can be constructed on any tonic or key note, all major scales have the same structure of whole-steps and half-steps. Therefore, in order to create major scales on notes other than *C*, we must use sharps or flats to get the half-steps in the right places. For instance, here is a *D* major scale (see Example 2). Without *F#* and *C#*, there would be half-steps between 2-3 and 6-7, and we would not have a major scale. The notes *F#* and *C#* are permanent parts of the scale of *D* major, and therefore permanent parts of the key of *D* major. We'll talk about this more when we discuss key signatures.

Each step in the scale has a name, which describes some aspect of that particular note's relationship to the key defined by that particular scale. Note 1 is, as we have said, the *tonic*—the note on which the scale is based. The next most important degree is the 5th, known as the *dominant*. Simply stated, the 5th degree is a dominant force in the scale and the key, both melodically and harmonically. The 3rd degree is the *mediant* so called because it is halfway between the tonic and the dominant. The tonic, mediant and dominant form the tonic triad, which is a major triad in the major scale.

The 4th degree is called the *subdominant*. You will notice that it is a fifth below the tonic, just as the dominant is a fifth above. It can be thought of as the "underneath dominant," or subdominant.

The 6th degree is the *submediant*—halfway between the tonic and the subdominant. The 2nd degree is the *supertonic*—the note above the tonic. And the 7th degree, since it has a strong melodic tendency to lead up to the tonic (if you're not sure about that, play a major scale and stop on the 7th degree), is called the *leading tone*.

To recapitulate: 1st step—tonic; 2nd step—supertonic; 3rd step—mediant; 4th step—subdominant; 5th step—dominant; 6th step—submediant; 7th step—leading tone. These terms are used a lot in traditional music theory; they are very useful when it comes to describing melodic and harmonic practice in tonal music.

Example 1.

Example 2.

Example 3.

Example 4.

Example 5.

Example 6.

Now on to the minor scale. If you have been made to practice scales, you probably know that there are *three* forms of the minor scale. Let's look at all three, and try to understand how this state of affairs came about. First, the natural minor scale (*A* minor scale) as illustrated in Example 3.

This is the minor scale that developed from the church modes. Note that the half-steps are between 2-3 and 5-6. Also notice that, because there is no half-step between 7-8, there is no leading tone relationship between the 7th scale degree and the tonic (by the way, when this leading tone relationship does not exist, the 7th degree is called *subtonic*). Back in the days when tonality was developing out of modality, musicians noticed this, too. The leading tone is a strong tool in the definition of tonality. Its melodic strength is obvious, but even more important is its harmonic role as the 3rd of the dominant triad. When the leading tone relationship is not present, the dominant triad is a minor chord (rather than a major chord) and the melodic motion of the leading tone within the chord is also lost. Therefore, it came to pass that many musicians raised the 7th degree when using the minor scale. Since this was done primarily for harmonic reasons, this scale has come to be known as *harmonic minor* (see Example 4).

Now we have half-steps between 2-3, 5-6, and 7-8; but we also have an augmented whole-step between 6-7! If you play this scale you'll notice that this particular step is not nearly as smooth as the others (melodically). Our early tonal musicians noticed this, too, and it occured to them to smooth things out again by raising the 6th degree also. In that way they would have the melodically (and harmonically) strong leading tone, but would also have smooth stepwise motion throughout the scale. Here we have an alteration done primarily for melodic reasons, so this scale has come to be known as *melodic minor* (see Example 5).

But wait—the strong *melodic* tendency of the leading tone is only operative when moving *up* to the tonic. When moving down, there is no strong melodic reason to alter the 7th degree to create a leading tone. Therefore, in the melodic minor scale, the 7th degree is returned to its original form on the way down; and, since the 7th degree is in its original form, there is no longer any reason to alter the 6th degree, so it returns to its original form, too. In other words, the descending form of melodic minor is just like natural minor (see Example 6).

So the ascending and descending forms of melodic minor are different. In *A* melodic minor, we have *F*♯ and *G*♯ on the way up, and *G*♮ and *F*♮ on the way down. And all three forms of the minor scale have a distinct structure: Natural minor has half-steps between 2-3 and 5-6; harmonic minor has half-steps between 2-3, 5-6, and 7-8, plus an augmented whole-step between 6-7; and melodic minor has half-steps beween 2-3 and 7-8 ascending, and between 2-3 and 5-6 descending.

Tom Darter

KEYS, AND KEY SIGNATURES

A piece of music is considered to be in a particular key if it uses one of the major or minor scales as a basis for its structure. The tonic of the scale is also the tonic (or key note) of the piece—the piece is said to be in that key. For instance, if a particular composition were based on structures derived from the C major scale, the piece would be said to be in the key of C major. If a composition were based on structures derived from the C minor scales, it would be said to be in the key of C minor. (By the way, this designation holds no matter which of the minor scales is being used—as a matter of fact, pieces in minor keys often make use of all the minor scale forms. There is no such thing as a piece in the key of C harmonic minor "C minor" covers the situation nicely.)

Music that is written using only the notes of a particular scale is called *diatonic* music. (*Diatonic* comes from two Greek words meaning "stretched through." Although the derivation is a bit oblique, this could be expanded to "stretched through the notes of the scale." In other words, the word *diatonic* has no hidden meaning—it simply means "the notes of the scale.") Notes that are not part of a particular scale are called *chromatic* relative to that scale. For instance, in the key of C major, the notes *C#, D#, F#, G#,* and *A#* are considered chromatic as in Example 1.

Example 1.

Example 2.

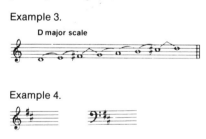

The word *chromatic* comes from the Greek word for "color." In one sense, chromatic notes do add color to the basic palette of diatonic notes. Also, by adding the chromatic tones of a particular key to the scale notes of that key, you would have all the notes in our equal-tempered system—all of the colors of our musical rainbow. By the way, if you construct a scale using all of the notes of the equal-tempered system, you have, appropriately enough, the chromatic scale (see Example 2).

Example 3.

Example 4.

In the key of C major (as shown above), it is easy to differentiate between the diatonics and chromatic notes: The notes without sharps or flats are diatonic in C major, while the notes with sharps (or flats) are chromatic. This makes reading music in the key of C major a very simple thing. (By the way, if you play some piano, or know a friend who does, you can get a good graphic understanding of diatonic and chromatic notes in the key of C major by simply looking at the keyboard: The white keys are diatonic in C major, and the black keys are chromatic.)

In other keys, however, the differentiation is not as straightforward. For instance, let's look at the D major scale and the key of D major. As we saw, it is necessary to use F# and C# in order to create the major scale structure on the key note *D* (see Example 3). Therefore, both *F#* and *C#* are diatonic notes in the key of *D* major. The chromatic notes in *D* major are *D#, G#, A#, F♮,* and *C♮.*

Since the notes *F#* and *C#* are diatonic in the key of *D* major, it would be necessary to indicate both with a sharp whenever they occur in the music; and, if you used chromatic pitches in your *D* major composition, they would also be indicated by sharps, flats, or naturals in front of particular notes. Now this could get confusing. Therefore, the early tonal musicians began indicating the sharps or flats that were diatonic (part of the scale) at the beginning of the piece. These indications are called *key signatures*, since they are characteristic for each key and scale. See Example 4 for the key signature for the key of *D* major. This means that whenever the notes *F* and *C* appear in the music, they automatically are raised to *F#* and *C#*, respectively, by the sharps indicated in the key signature. In order to have *F♮*, you need to use a natural sign in front of the *F*, to cancel out the sharp in the key signature.

As you can see, the use of key signatures has a number of advantages. One of the most important is that the sharps, flats and naturals that you encounter in the course of a piece of music are *all* chromatic pitches in the key, since the sharps or flats needed to create the diatonic scale are indicated in the key signatures.

So key signatures are very useful, and they are used consistently in tonal music. But of course that means that in order to deal successfully with tonal music, you need to know the key signature associated with each key. Don't worry though, it doesn't involve a lot of random memorization—there is a definite pattern involved in the various major key signatures. As we begin to go through them, the patterns will emerge; and once you learn the patterns, it becomes very easy to learn all of the major key signatures.

Let's start with *C* major: The scale of *C* major has no sharps or flats, so the key signature of *C* major has no sharps or flats. Simple enough.

In order to build a major scale on *G*, the note *F#* is necessary (to create the half-step between notes 7-8 in the scale), so *F#* is a permanent part of the scale and the key of *G* major (and is indicated in the key signature). Here is the scale signature for *G* major (see Example 5).

Example 5.

We have already mentioned the scale and key of *D* major—two sharps are needed, *F#* and *C#* (see Example 6).

Example 6.

Already we can see some patterns. *G* major has one sharp, *F#*, and it applies to the 7th note of the scale. In *D* major there are two sharps: *F#* (the same sharp found in *G* major) and *C#* (which applies to the 7th note of the scale). Now, if this is indeed a pattern, we should expect the scale with three sharps to have *F#, C#,* and another sharp, which will apply to the 7th note of the scale. As it turns out, the scale and key of *A* major fits the bill nicely (see Example 7).

Example 7.

Now we can see another pattern, relative to the tonic note of these keys: *C* major—no sharps (or flats); *G* major—one sharp; *D* major—two sharps; *A* major—three sharps. You will notice that each successive key note is a perfect fifth higher than the previous key note. Therefore, we should expect that the key with four sharps should be *E* major, since *E* is a perfect fifth above *A*. And the sharps should be *F#, C#, G#* (all three of which have shown up in our previous keys) plus *D#*—which applies to the 7th note of the *E* scale. Once again, all of the patterns work.

Example 8.

Continuing with our pattern, we find that *B* major has five sharps (our old friends *F#, C#, G#,* and *D#,* plus *A#*), *F#* major has six sharps (*F#, C#, G#, D#, A#,* and *E#*), and *C#* major has seven sharps (a sharp in front of every note, with *B#* being the new sharp).

So we have discovered that all of the major keys that use sharps in their key signature are related by pattern. The key notes are related by ascending perfect fifths as the number of sharps goes up (*C* major, *G* major, *D* major, *A* major, *E* major, *B* major, *F#* major, and so on). Also, the sharps themselves have a pattern. In order of appearance they are *F#, C#, G#, D#, A#, E#, B#*. This order of appearance is reflected in the positioning of the sharps in the key signature. The sharps always appear in this position and order in key signatures (see Example 8).

Here are the key signatures of all the keys we have discussed so far (see Example 9).

Example 9.

Now that we have covered the key signatures involving sharps, it's time to move on to those that involve flats. By now you should not be surprised to discover that there are patterns in operation here too. Just as the sharp keys are related by ascending perfect fifths, the flat keys are related by *descending* perfect fifths; *C* major—no flats (or sharps); *F* major—one flat; *Bb* major—two flats; *Eb* major—three flats; *Ab* major—four flats; *Db* major—five flats; *Gb* major–six flats; and *Cb* major—seven flats.

There is also a pattern in the appearance of the flats. The one flat in the key of *F* major is *Bb*. As you can see, it applies to the 4th note of the scale (see Example 10).

Example 10.

In the key of *Bb* major, the two flats involved are *Bb* plus *Eb* (and *Eb* once again applies to the 4th note of the scale). (See Example 11).

Example 11.

So there is a pattern in the appearance of the flats, too, and this pattern is reflected in the positioning of the flats in the key signature.

Here are the key signatures for all of the basic keys involving flats. Notice how the patterns work (see Example 12).

Example 12.

Once you learn the patterns that bind together the various major scales, key signatures are easy to learn.

Example 13.

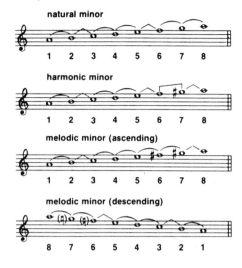

Example 14.

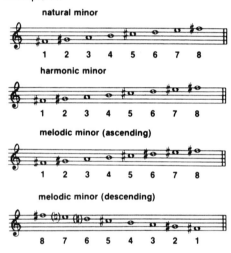

There is a slightly different situation at work in the minor keys because each minor key has at least *three* scales that form the basis for its structure.

The three minor scales that are used with regularity in tonal music are natural minor (with half-steps between notes 2-3 and 5-6), harmonic minor (with half-steps between notes 2-3, 5-6, and 7-8, plus an augmented whole-step between 6-7), and melodic minor (with half-steps between 2-3 and 7-8 when ascending, and half-steps between 2-3 and 5-6 when descending). Here are the scales involved in the key of *A* minor (see Example 13).

You will notice that the *A* natural minor scale uses no sharps or flats, while the other two *A* minor scales use sharps (and naturals). So, how do we go about determining the key signature for this (and all other) minor keys? The answer is that the only sharps or flats that belong in a minor key signature are those that all three scale forms have in common. Since the harmonic minor and melodic minor scales were derived from the natural minor scale, it can be thought of as the scale that provides the basis for the key structure (and the key signature indication). Therefore, the key signature for the key of *A* minor involves no sharps or flats. In order to create the harmonic minor or melodic minor scale forms in *A* minor (or in any other minor key), accidentals must be used.

So, the key of *A* minor has the same key signature as the key of *C* major. The key notes of the two keys are related by a minor third. Could this relationship indicate another set of patterns in the key structure of tonal music? Let's look at another set of keys and find out.

The key of *A* major involves three sharps (*F#*, *C#*, and *G#*). If there is indeed a pattern involved, we would expect the key of *F#* minor (a minor third down) to include the same three sharps. Here are the three minor scale forms built up from *F#* (see example 14). As you see, the only sharps that the three scale forms have in common are *F#*, *C#*, and *G#*. The pattern holds.

And so every key signature does double duty—it defines the structure of one major key and one minor key. In every case the key note of the minor key involved is a minor third lower than the key note of the major key. Since there is such an obvious relationship between the two keys that share the same key signature, they are said to be *relative*. Thus, *A* minor is the relative minor of *C* major, and *C* major is the relative major of *A* minor. Example 14 shows the key signatures for all of the basic major and minor keys (major keys are listed above the staff, with their relative minors listed below):

What about the relationship between *A* major and *A* minor? Well, since they share the same note, they are referred to as being *parallel*. So *A* major is the parallel major of *A* minor, and *A* minor is the parallel minor of *A* major. If you look at the key signatures above, you will notice that every minor key has three fewer sharps (or three more flats, or some combination of the two) than its parallel major. One way to remember this is to think of sharps as positive numbers and flats as negative numbers—then the difference between a minor key and its parallel major can always be thought of as 3 (simply). For example: The key of *G* minor has two flats (–2), and its parallel major has one sharp (–2 + 3 =1).

Tom Darter

THE CIRCLE OF FIFTHS

Now that we have discussed the basic major and minor keys and key signatures, it's time to take a look at the circle of fifths. It provides a straight-forward graphic display of patterns and relationships to be found in the key structure of tonal music, and it also has a number of other uses.

The major keys that use sharps in their key signatures are found by moving around the circle in a clockwise direction beginning from C at the top, while the major keys that use flats are found by moving around the cirle from C on a counterclockwise direction. You will remember that the sharp keys are related by ascending perfect fifths (as the number of sharps increases), while the flat keys are related by descending perfect fifths (as the number of flats increases). These relationships are shown directly on the circle.

The relative minor keys are displayed in the same way on the inner circle of fifths diagram (see Figure 1). To find the relative minor of a particular major key, just move along the radial line to the inner circle. Likewise, to find the relative major of a particular key, move along the radial line to the outer circle. The number of sharps or flats on the key signature of each key is shown in the center of the circle, at the end of each connecting radial line.

It's easy to find parallel keys and their signatures on the circle, too. To find the parallel minor of a particular major key, just move three positions around the circle in a counterclockwise direction and look to the inner circle. To find the parallel major of a particular minor key, move three positions around the circle in a clockwise direction and look to the outer circle. As you can see, the +3/−3 relationship discussed earlier is represented graphically in the circle of fifths.

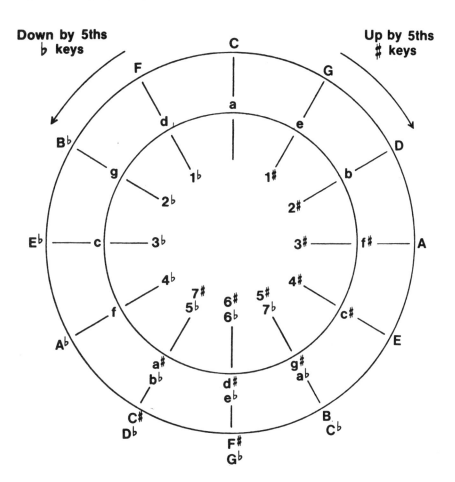

Down by 5ths
♭ **keys**

Up by 5ths
♯ **keys**

In case you need to refresh your memory on the order of appearance of sharps of flats in the basic key signatures, the circle can help. Notice that the seven basic note names (*C, D, E, F, G, A, B*) are shown on a row on the outer circle of the diagram. If you begin at *F* and move around the circle clockwise (the sharp direction), you will find the order of appearance of the sharps in the sharp key signatures (*F-C-G-D-A-E-B*). If you begin at the other end with *B* and move around the circle counterclockwise (the flat direction), you will find the order of appearance of the flats in the flat key signatures (*B-E-A-D-G-C-F*).

At the bottom of the diagram, you will notice that certain of the sharp and flat keys overlap—for instance, the key of *F♯* major (six sharps) occupies the same position as the key of *G♭* major (six flats). You will also notice that if you play the scale of *F♯* major on the guitar followed by the scale of *G♭* major, you will be playing the same notes. The notes *F♯* and *G♭* are called *enharmonic equivalents*, and in our system of equal temperament they sound exactly the same—it follows that the scales built up from these two notes would also be enharmonically equivalent. The subject of enharmonic equivalents is an important one (particularly as it relates to different systems of temperament); we'll discuss this later.

Now that we've covered the basic relationships shown in the circle, let's close by looking at the reason for putting all of this information in a circle to begin with. If you play the indicated notes around the circle in either direction, you will find an uninterrupted chain of perfect fifths that always returns to its own starting place (keep in mind that this involves the use of an enharmonic spelling change at some point, and that it only works directly in our system of equal temperament). This continuous cycle (often referred to as the cycle of fifths), besides showing the overall relationship of the 15 basic major keys, is useful in understanding the structure of certain kinds of chord progressions (among other things).

All in all, the circle of fifths is a very useful tool!

Tom Darter

RHYTHMIC NOTATION

So far we have been talking about the basic priciples involved in the relationships between pitches in our traditional system of notation: scales, intervals, triads, keys, and key signatures. Before we move on to a discussion of tonal harmony and chord progression, we're going to take a look at another area of music fundamentals that often gets lost in the shuffle to learn about altered 13th chords. The notation of rhythm and meter has evolved in our traditional system alongside the notation of pitch, and a thorough understanding of it is just as vital to any musician who ever has to deal with notated music.

In simple terms, our rhythmic notation is based on a set of symbols that indicate relative duration (of both notes and rests). By themselves, these symbols only indicate the duration of a note relative to the duration of another (for instance, a half note lasts twice as long as a quarter note). In order to translate these symbols into something concrete, a reference point must be given. That is where meter comes in. A meter tells the musician what kind of note lasts a beat, and tells how many of those beats

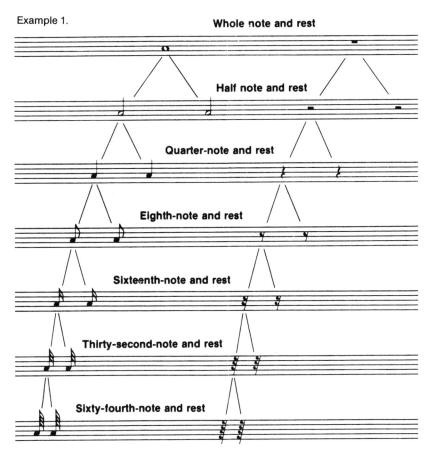

Example 1.

Example 2.

Example 3.

there will be in any given bar of music. The duration of a beat is then given, either in a relative way with a tempo indication (*allegro*, for example, which means "fast"), or in a specific way with a metronome marking.

However, in order to know how to deal with the reference points provided by metrical and metronome markings, it is necessary to know how the system of relative duration markings works. The basic set of duration indications (both for note values and rests) is given in the Example 1. You will notice that all of the basic proportions involved are multiples of two; two quarter notes equal one half note. Two eighth-notes equal one quarter note, and so on. By the way, remember that these are all relative durations. Quite often (since the quarter note is the reference point for the beat in a number of common meters) people get the impression that quarter notes are "one-beat notes." But on occasion, half notes, eighth-notes, or, more rarely, sixteenth-notes might be designated as constituting the basic beat.

So this is a pretty simple set of symbols; and since they are all based on multiples of two, they would seem to be limited in terms of notating more complex rhythmic shapes. For this reason, other symbols are used to increase the flexibility of the system. The most basic of these is the dot. Once again, the dot is an indication of relative duration—when placed after a note it adds half the value of the note to the note (the same holds true for rests). It is the equivalent of adding the next lower note value to the note that has the dot (see Example 2). So a dotted half note is equal to three quarter notes.

On occasion you will also see doubly-dotted notes or rests. The second dot adds half the value of the first dot to the note (see Example 3).

So a doubly-dotted quarter note is equal to three-and-a-half eighth-notes, or seven sixteenth-notes. And, as you can see, all of the durations involved are relative.

Tom Darter

METERS AND TIME SIGNATURES

Example 1.

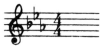

Example 2.

Example 3.

We've now gone over the fundamentals of our standard system of rhythmic notation, and seen that all durations are indicated in a relative way. In order to provide a frame of reference for the rhythms indicated, we need two things: (1) a meter, which tells us what kind of note gets a beat and how many beats there are in a measure of music; and (2) a tempo or metronome indication, which tells us the duration of a beat. Let's look at some of the basic principles used in the notation of meter.

Meters are indicated at the beginning of a piece of music with a time signature (or meter signature), which is written right after the clef indication and the key signature (see Example 1). As you can see, the time signature consists of two numbers, one on top of the other. The bottom number indicates (directly or indirectly) the note value of the beat, while the top number indicates (directly or indirectly) the number of beats in a measure of music. (By the way, since measures are separated by bar lines, the word *bar* is often used interchangeably with the word *measure*.) The only numbers you will ever find as the bottom number in a time signature will be multiples of two: 1, 2, 4, 8, 16, and sometimes even 32 or 64. If 4 is the bottom number, that means that a quarter note gets the beat; if 2 is the bottom number, a half note gets the beat; if 16 is the bottom note, a sixteenth-note gets the beat.

Strictly speaking, there can be any number of beats in a bar of music, but certain numbers are much more common than others. For now we will look at the meters that are called *regular* meters—those that have two, three, or four beats to the measure.) Meters with five or more beats to the measure are called *irregular meters*; we will discuss those in a later column. And yes, there is a name for each of these kinds of meter: A meter with two beats per bar is called a *duple* meter; a meter with three beats per bar is called a *triple* meter; and one with four beats per bar is called a *quadruple* meter.

There is one other element we need to look at to complete the picture—the background unit, which is the note value representing the largest possible subdivision of a single beat (see Example 2). Here we have a triple meter with the quarter note getting the beat. The background unit is the eighth-note—it subdivides the beat into two parts.

However, there is another set of regular meters, ones in which the basic beat is subdivided into three parts by the background unit. The problem is that since we don't have a basic note value that is equal to three of another note, we can't indicate the note value of the beat directly in the time signature. (Of course, dotted note values are equal to three of another note, but they cannot be indicated by a single number—we have no such thing as a "third-note" or a "ninth-note.")

Therefore, for meters of this kind, the time signature indicates the basic background unit of the meter, and tells us how many background units there are in a measure. Here is a triple meter of this type (see Example 3). The note that is actually getting the beat here is the dotted quarter note, and the beat is subdivided into three parts by the background unit (the eighth-note). Since the time signature indicates the meter only indirectly, and since the basic subdivision of the beat is into three parts, meters of this type are called *compound meters*. Meters in which the basic subdivision of the beat is into two parts are called *simple meters*.

One last thing: Although it is common to repeat the key signature on each line of a piece of music, the time signature is found only at the beginning of the first line (unless, of course, the meter changes during the course of the piece).

Tom Darter

RHYTHM VS. METER: SYNCOPATION

So far in our discussion of rhythmic notation and its relationship to meter, we have spoken of the various meters only in terms of their function as a grid (or framework) for our systems of relative duration. However, meters do much more than provide us with a simple frame of reference for the determination of tempo: In traditional notated music, a meter implies a certain type of rhythmic structure, one that works in each measure of the music. The basic form of the metrical structure is found at the level of the beat, which can be thought of as strong or weak.

The first beat is always the most important in the structure of any meter—it carries with it an implicit accent (the word *implicit* is important here). The other beats are relatively weaker (in *structural* importance). Figure 1 is a graphic representation of the beat structure of the regular meters (a slash indicates more emphasis, a ∪ indicates less). You will notice that quadruple meter has a secondary implicit accent on the third beat. Implicit accents can fall on or between beats. For instance, in any simple meter where a quarter note gets the beat, implicit accents can be found within a grouping of four sixteeth-notes. This meter (on a much smaller level; see Example 1). The levels of these implicit patterns follow a strict hierarchy: The level of the beat is always more important than any subdivision of the beat. Therefore, the second beat in a quadruple meter, although thought of as a "weak" beat, is more important (by which I mean that it receives more implicit accent) than any implicit "strong" note value functioning within a division of any beat. These implicit accent patterns function up and down the structure of our regular meter system.

Of course, not all rhythmic patterns fall neatly within this very rigid structure of implicit accents. Most rhythmic patterns go counter to these basic metric patterns. One of the major elements of rhythmic interest in metric music involves precisely this tension between the implied accent pattern of the meter and the actual rhythmic patterns operating within the meter. Any type of rhythmic pattern that operates contrary to the basic metric structure in which it is articulated is called *syncopation*. (This word derives from the Medieval Latin word *syncopare*, meaning "to cut short." You can think of a syncopation as a rhythmic pattern that cuts against the grain of the basic metric structure.) Here are two simple examples of syncopation in 4/4 meter (See Examples 2 and 3). As you can see, these rhythmic patterns do not directly articulate the beat structure of the meter, they cut across the beat structure, creating implicit accents of their own.

In both of the above examples, I have indicated the syncopations by using ties so that the basic beat structure would be easy to visualize. In actual practice, simple syncopations such as these are quite often notated without the use of ties (see Examples 4 and 5).

When notated this way, the third beat can no longer be seen directly in either example; but it is unlikely that many people would lose their bearings within the bar.

However, when more complicated syncopations occur, ties and/or beams are often used in order to maintain (in the notation itself) the implicit structure of the meter. Thus, a player can continually orient himself or herself to that constant metrical background. Take a look at the rhythmic notation in Example 6.

Here we have a complicated syncopation pattern. It is beamed so that the third beat can be seen, but the second and fourth beats are completely obscured. Now look at Example 7.

The example exactly duplicates the rhythmic pattern of Example 6, but it is notated (using beams and ties) so that all four beats can be easily visualized by the player. If I were sight-reading, I would much rather be looking at the second version. Wouldn't you?

Here is one more illustration of the usefulness of clear rhythmic notation—this time in a compound meter (see Examples 8 and 9).

Figure 1.

duple: / ∪

triple: / ∪ ∪

quadruple: / ∪ / ∪

Example 1.

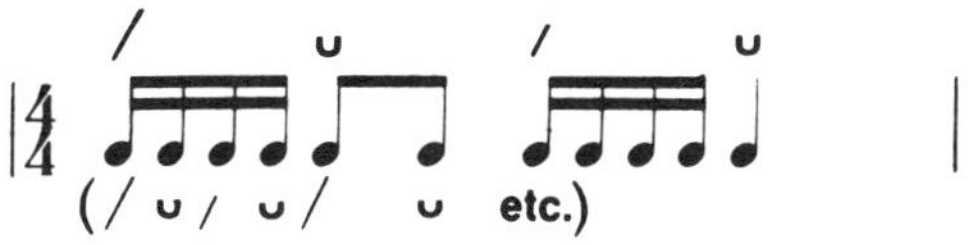

Example 2.

Example 3.

Example 4.

Example 5.

Example 6.

Example 7.

Example 8.

Example 9.

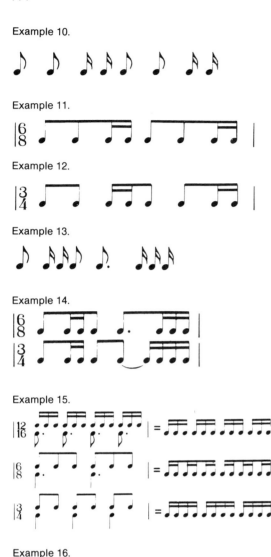

Example 10.

Example 11.

Example 12.

Example 13.

Example 14.

Example 15.

Example 16.

Once again, both examples are notations of the same rhythmic pattern. In Example 8, no ties are used, and all of the note values smaller than a quarter note are beamed together arbitrarily. As a result, the beat structure of the meter is visually obscured. In Example 9, beams and ties are used to clarify the underlying metric structure—all three beats can be seen (and felt), even if they are not articulated directly by the rhythmic pattern itself. And once again, I would much rather look at (and play from) the second version.

Using ties and beams, we can also notate syncopations is such a way that their relationship to a basic metric structure remains clear (visually and conceptually) throughout any complex pattern occuring within a beat or over a set of beats.

All of this makes it very easy for players to orient themselves to the constant background structure provided by the meter. However, the value of keeping a clear outline of the meter in the notation of a rhythm extends far beyond that of keeping your place: the basic structure of a meter, although only implicit in the way most rhythms are constructed, will almost always make a difference in the way a particular rhythm is played (in traditional notated music). For instance, look at the rhythmic pattern in Example 10. It is very easy to tap out this pattern. As it stands, you would probably tend to assume that it was in 6/8 time, because the pattern itself (in the abstract) seems to express the basic patterns of 6/8. The standard way to beam this pattern is 6/8 as shown in Example 11.

However, it would also be possible for this rhythmic pattern to exist in a bar of 3/4 meter. It would then be beamed so that the metric pattern would be easy to visualize (see Example 12).

This rhythmic pattern is fairly straightforward in both meters—there are no syncopations, no ties, and no unusual durations. Nevertheless, you will notice that there will be a subtle difference in the way you play the two examples (even though the rhythmic patterns are in the abstract, the same), based on your implicit understanding of the metric structures of the two meters.

Another abstract rhythmic pattern is shown in Example 13. The same pattern, notated in 6/8 meter and in 3/4 meter is shown in Example 14.

You will notice that the dotted eighth-note has a completely different meaning in the two metric examples: In the 6/8 example it falls on the second beat of the duple meter, and therefore emphasizes (and reinforces) the implicit metrical accent; in the 3/4 example the dotted eighth-note works as a syncopation, cutting across the third beat of the triple meter and working contrary to the implicit accent pattern of the meter.

To give you one more example of the importance of metric structure as it relates to the feel of a particular rhythmic pattern, let's look at three different meters, all of which contains the same number of sixteenth-notes in one bar (see Example 15).

Example 17.

The first meter, 12/16, is a compound quadruple meter, and the proper grouping (or beaming) of sixteenth-notes would be in threes—they represent the basic subdivision of the beat. The second meter is 6/8, a compound duple meter; the sixteenth-notes are grouped (or beamed) in twos and/or sixes—in this case they represent a further subdivision of the basic subdivision of the beat. The third example is 3/4, a simple triple meter; in this case the sixteenth-notes would be grouped in fours, representing (once again) a subdivision of the basic subdivision of eighth-notes.

Now, here is an abstract rhythmic pattern that has a total duration of 12 sixteenth-notes (see Example 16).

Once again, this is an easy pattern to tap out, and if represented in the abstract like this it should probably be tapped out (played) without any implicit accents at all. Example 17 is the same pattern as it would be notated in the three meters that were shown in Example 15.

Establish the structure of each meter in your mind and play through each example (either tapping on a table top or playing one note on your guitar). You will see that, although the relative durations are the same across all three examples, the relationship of the rhythmic pattern to the implicit structure of the meter is different in each case—there will be a subtle difference in the feel of the rhythm (as played and as heard) in each meter. You will also notice that in each case the rhythm is notated so that the structure of the meter remains visually clear.

Tom Dorter

RHYTHMIC NOTATION: TIES AND BEAMS

An important element in the traditional system of rhythmic notation is the tie. The tie looks exactly like a slur mark or a phrase mark, but a tie always connects two notes of the same pitch. The tie allows us to create written note durations (relative durations, as always) that can't be achieved with just the basic aggregation of note symbols and dots. Let's look at relative durations that are multiples of an eighth-note duration. We can show values of one, two, and four eighth-notes using the basic duration symbols discussed earlier (eighth-note, quarter note, and half note, respectively); and we can show values of three, six, and seven eighth-notes using duration symbols and dots (dotted quarter, dotted half, and doubly-dotted half); however, to indicate a duration of five eighth-notes we must use a tie (for instance, a half note tied to an eighth-note). Example 1 illustrates the complete set of duration multiples we have just mentioned, arranged in order of relative length.

Another important use of the tie is to notate durations that last longer than a single bar of music. For instance, if you wanted to notate a duration of ten beats within a 3/4 meter, the tie would be used as in Example 2.

Obviously the tie must be used in order to notate durations that extend from one bar to another (since the notes in any one bar must add up to the number of beats indicated in the time signature). For example, an abstract rhythmic pattern is illustrated in Example 3. If you want to notate this pattern in a 2/4 meter, you would have to do something like that shown in Example 4. As you see, the note values that extend over the bar lines are split apart according to the structure of the measure, and their existence as a single-note duration is then indicated with a tie. (By the way, ties are never used to tie rest values together. Since rests require no articulation, a lengthy silence can be indicated by a string of rest symbols.)

Another important procedure in our traditional system of rhythmic notation involves the beaming together of two or more note symbols that

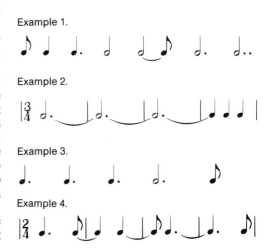

Example 1.

Example 2.

Example 3.

Example 4.

use flags (eighth-notes, sixteenth-notes, thirty-second-notes, and so on). The beams replace the flags, as follows (see Example 5).

Example 5.

Beams are usually use to form note groups that coincide with the beat patterns of the meter. For instance, a group of four sixteenth-notes would be found in a meter where a quarter note gets a beat (2/4, 3/4, 4/4), while a group of two sixteenth-notes might be found in a meter where a quarter note gets a beat (2/8, 3/8, 4/8). It is also possible to combine different note values of this type (including dotted note values) in various beamed note groupings (see Example 6).

Example 6.

Once again, these groupings would usually be made to coincide with some aspect of the beat structure. (You will notice that some of these examples involve the use of a kind of half beam. Unlike the flag it replaces, which always extends from the right side of the note stem, the half beam always remains inside the overall grouping provided by the top beam. If the half beam is used to indicate a shorter value that is associated with a dotted value or other larger value to form a sub-group, the half beam extends in the direction of that related larger value. Study the examples to see how this works).

All of the examples are likely to be found in simple meters (where the basic subdivision of the beat is into two parts). Beam groups can also be found in compound meters (where the basic division of the beat is into three parts). (See Example 7.)

Example 7.

You have seen that it is sometimes useful and important to divide certain notes connected with a tie in order to maintain the visual structure of the meter. This technique is also important in the notation of rest values (see Examples 8 and 9).

Example 8.   Example 9.

In Example 8, the second beat cannot be seen—it falls in the middle of the quarter rest. In Example 9, the quarter rest has been divided into two eighth-rests, and the second beat has a visual presence (remember, no ties are needed for combinations of rests).

Sometimes this redivision of rest values involves beamed-note values as well (see Example 10).

Example 10.

Example 11.

Here the eighth-rest on the left has been converted into two sixteenth-rests on the right so that the second beat remains visually clear. Other renotations occur later in the bar.

In Example 10, you will notice that the rest has been notated so that it is almost part of the beamed group of sixteenth-notes. This is done for visual clarity. Actually, there are a number of accepted ways to notate a group of beamed notes plus rests (see Example 11).

All three of these versions are perfectly clear: I prefer that last one because it retains the greatest visual clarity in terms of the beam structure as it relates to the meter.

Tom Darter

THE TRANSPOSITION CHART

Even the most difficult chords and chord progressions can be easily played if put into a more comfortable key. The accompanying transposition chart can be learned in a few minutes, and will give you the knowledge to play in any key desired.

Transposition is simply taking a musical idea, like a melody or chord progression and moving it to another key. The three chords in a tonic-dominant-subdominant progression have a definite relationship to each other. The tonic chord is built on the first degree of the major scale, the dominant is built on the fifth and the sub-dominant on the fourth. As long as this 1-5-4 relationship is maintained, you will always have the same chord progression no matter which of the 12 key scales you are using. For example, the Eb progression (Eb, C minor, Ab, Bb) is more easily played in the key of C where the chords are then C, A minor, F, G.

To make a transposition chart, first construct a horizontal line with the 12 basic notes in chromatic order (going up in half-steps, or one fret at a time on the guitar), beginning with C. (See accompanying chart.)

Next, make another horizontal line directly below it, beginning with the second note, Db. This sequence is repeated until you have 12 lines completed.

When using this chart to transpose a chord progression, you are only concerned with the root name of the chord. A minor chord will always transpose to a minor chord. A 7th, 9th, 11th, etc., will always transpose to a 7th, 9th, 11th, and so on. Only the root letter name of the chord will change in the transposition process.

First, recognize the key you are in, then locate the horizontal line which begins with that letter. (The key is usually named by the first or last chord in the progression.) Let's say your chord progression is F, G minor, Bb, C7: you are playing in the key of F. Let's also assume that the F chord is hard for you to play, the G minor is impossible, and you've never even heard of Bb. You need the same progression, but in a key with easier chords. D is a good key with many easy chords, so let's try it in D.

Find the F line and circle F, G, Bb, C, which are the root names of the chords in the key of F used in this progression. Next, locate the line starting with D—your new key. Since F is your key chord in the key of F, D

C	Db	D	Eb	E	F	Gb	G	Ab	A	Bb	B
Db	D	Eb	E	F	Gb	G	Ab	A	Bb	B	C
[D]	Eb	[E]	F	Gb	[G]	Ab	[A]	Bb	B	C	Db
Eb	E	F	Gb	G	Ab	A	Bb	B	C	Db	D
E	F	Gb	G	Ab	A	Bb	B	C	Db	D	Eb
(F)	Gb	(G)	Ab	A	(Bb)	B	(C)	Db	D	Eb	E
Gb	G	Ab	A	Bb	B	C	Db	D	Eb	E	F
G	Ab	A	Bb	B	C	Db	D	Eb	E	F	Gb
Ab	A	Bb	B	C	Db	D	Eb	E	F	Gb	G
A	Bb	B	C	Db	D	Eb	E	F	Gb	G	Ab
Bb	B	C	Db	D	Eb	E	F	Gb	G	Ab	A
B	C	Db	D	Eb	E	F	Gb	G	Ab	A	Bb

will be your new key chord; so F transposes to D. Your next chord in the key of F was G minor. So if you go horizontally from the D line, and up vertically from the circled G, you will intersect at E. Thus, G minor becomes E minor when transposed to the key of D. If you continue the process of going horizontally from the new key and up from the old chord, the lines will always intersect at the root name of the new chord.

Therefore, your new progression would be D, E minor, G, A7. You can now apply your knowledge of the 12 basic tones to make an easy transposition chart from memory.

If your chord knowledge is weak, or if you are teaching someone whose is, you can use the chart to greatly simplify the chords in many cases.

ABOUT THE AUTHORS

Jim Aikin is a former assistant editor of *Guitar Player* and has been an editor for *Keyboard* since in 1975. Jim began his musical career as a classical cellist, but went on to play electric bass in rock bands.

Bob Baxter has been involved in music education for many years. He has written more than a dozen guitar instruction books and headed his own music school in Santa Monica, CA. He also hosted the CBS Television series, "Baxter's Guitar Workshop."

Jeff Baxter is best known for his work with Steely Dan and the Doobie Brothers. He has been playing rock guitar since the age of 10 and is also an accomplished steel guitar player. Since leaving the Doobie Brothers, he has concentrated on studio work and tinkering with his guitars.

Michael Brooks is a former assistant editor of *Guitar Player*.

Tom Darter has been the Editor of *Keyboard* magazine since its birth in 1975. He is also an eminent performer, composer and teacher.

Rik Emmett is known to millions of rock music fans as the imaginative, virtuosic lead guitarist for the Canadian power trio, Triumph. He has had numerous essays, critiques, and guest columns in the magazines and dailies of Toronto, his home base.

Jim Ferguson is an assistant editor for *Guitar Player* and an accomplished jazz and classical guitarist. As a freelance writer, his work has appeared in many publications. He has also written notes for albums by Jim Hall, Tal Farlow, and Charlie Byrd.

Stefan Grossman is a musician, composer, author, teacher, and record producer with numerous books and records to his credit. He has published definitive fingerpicking texts for Oak Publications and more than a dozen albums under his own name. He is considered a primary source on black American blues guitarists, having studied with Rev. Gary Davis, Mississippi John Hurt, Skip James, Fred McDowell, and Son House.

Barney Kessel is an internationally renowned jazz guitarist who has performed and recorded with dozens of consequential jazz musicians over the past three decades. He is also a gifted teacher and writer with several guitar instruction books to his credit.

B.B. King is the King of the Blues. His legendary approach to the guitar has affected countless guitarists of all musical idioms.

Michael Lorimer is one of the world's leading classical guitarists as well as a teacher, transcriber, and scholar. He has studied with Andres Segovia and was the first American classical guitarist invited to perform in the Soviet Union.

Don Menn has been associated with *Guitar Player* since 1973, rising from editorial assistant to Editor in 1978. He has been Associate Publisher of GPI Publications since July 1981.

Tom Mulhern is associate editor for *Guitar Player* and has been with GPI Publications since 1977.

Les Paul has been performing professionally for more than 50 years and is the remarkable genius behind sound-on-sound overdubbing and multiple-track recording. He was a pioneer of the solidbody guitar and, along with his wife Mary Ford, was one of the world's biggest stars in the 1950s.

Lee Ritenour, at 32, has already worked in a wider variety of musical situations than most players do in a lifetime. For five years he was one of Hollywood's premier studio guitarists, appearing on more than 200 albums and some of the best-selling soundtracks in history (e.g. *Saturday Night Fever* and *Grease*). For the past few years he has concentrated on a performing career and has recorded a number of successful albums with his own band.

Jon Sievert is the staff photographer for GPI Publications and has authored numerous articles for *Guitar Player, Frets,* and *Keyboard*.

Jerry Silverman is known throughout the guitar world as an instrumentalist and teacher of many styles—especially beginning and intermediate folk, blues and rock. He is also an accomplished author with many popular method books and anthologies to his credit.

Johnny Smith is a legendary jazz guitarist who gave up the traveling life of a performing musician nearly 30 years ago. During the early '50s he won virtually every jazz guitar poll in sight and then retired to his Colorado Springs home to teach the instrument.

Jimmy Stewart is a Hollywood studio guitarist, arranger, conductor, and recording artist. He is also a teacher and has authored a book on classical guitar for Guitar Player Books.

Happy Traum is a well-known acoustic guitarist, teacher and author with many instruction books to his credit. He is also the founder and president of Homespun Tapes, which specializes in music instruction.

Other Titles in the Guitar Player Basic Library:

ROCK GUITAR

 B.B. King, Lee Ritenour, Jeff Baxter, Larry Coryell, Arlen Roth, Rik Emmett, Jimmy Stewart, Bruce Bergman, Rick Derringer, Jim Aikin, and other outstanding working guitar players and teachers present a comprehensive approach to learning and performing the different styles of rock guitar. Compiled from the pages of Guitar Player Magazine, the most respected publication in the field today.

73999-00689-00294 $8.95
ISBN 0-88188-294-1

ELECTRIC BASS GUITAR

 Carol Kaye, Chuck Rainey, Stanley Clarke, Herb Mickman, Jeff Berlin, Michael Brooks, Andy West, Ken Smith, and other outstanding working bassists and bass teachers present a definitive approach to the theory, practice, and performance of electric bass guitar. From the pages of Guitar Player Magazine.

73999-00689-00292 $8.95
ISBN 0-88188-292-5

HL HAL LEONARD PUBLISHING CORPORATION